James Bond on Location

Volume 2: U.K.
(excluding London)

J. P. Sperati

All correspondence for
**James Bond on Location
Volume 2: U.K. (excluding London)**
should be addressed to:

Irregular Special Press
Endeavour House
170 Woodland Road
Sawston
Cambridge
CB22 3DX

✵✵✵✵✵ ◯ ✵✵✵✵✵

Copyright © 2013 Baker Street Studios Limited
All rights reserved
Typesetting is in Times New Roman font

ISBN: 1-901091-58-9 (10 digit)
ISBN: 978-1-901091-58-8 (13 digit)

| Deluxe full colour edition also available
ISBN: 1-901091-57-0 (10 digit)
ISBN: 978-1-901091-57-1 (13 digit) |

Proof reading & editing: Roger Johnson
Front cover concept: Stephen Norris
Back cover: One of the Aston Martins used in filming *Skyfall* at Glencoe

✵✵✵✵✵ ◯ ✵✵✵✵✵

All rights reserved. No part of this publication may be reproduced, stored in a retrieval system, or transmitted, in any form or by any means, electronic, mechanical, photocopying, recording or otherwise, without the prior permission of the Irregular Special Press.

✵✵✵✵✵ ◯ ✵✵✵✵✵

This publication is not part of the official James Bond series. It has not been endorsed or authorised by EON, Danjaq, LLC, United Artists Corporation, Columbia Pictures Industries, Sony or MGM. It does not claim or imply any rights to the Ian Fleming characters or creations and is a historical review of those locations already in the public domain used in filming the James Bond series. Film titles, character names and other information that might be copyright protected are used for reference only.

✵✵✵✵✵ ◯ ✵✵✵✵✵

Every effort has been made to ensure accuracy, but the publishers do not hold themselves responsible for any consequences that may arise from errors or omissions. Whilst the contents are believed to be correct at the time of going to press, changes may have occurred since that time or will occur during the currency of this publication.

**For James,
James A. E. R.**

CONTENTS

Introduction 9

James Bond in England 13

James Bond in Bedfordshire 15
Luton – Luton Hoo 15
Millbrook – Millbrook Proving Ground 17

James Bond in Berkshire 21
Ascot – Ascot Racecourse 21
Hurley – Hurley Lock 24
Wraysbury – Wraysbury Lake 26

James Bond in Buckinghamshire 29
Beaconsfield – Royal Saracen's Head Hotel 29
Black Park 31
Burnham Beeches 37
Denham – Denham Quarry Lakes 39
Gerrards Cross – Chalfont Park House 41
Halton – Halton House 42
Iver Heath – Pinewood Studios 45
Marlow – Thames Lawn 56
Newport Pagnell – Aston Martin Works 58
Oakley – R.A.F. Oakley 62
Stoke Poges – St. Giles' Church, Stoke Park 64
Stowe – Stowe Landscape Gardens 69
Waddesdon – Waddesdon Manor 72

James Bond in Cambridgeshire 75
Wansford – Nene Valley Railway 75

James Bond in Cornwall 89
Bodelva – Eden Project 89
Newquay – Holywell Bay 91

James Bond in East Sussex 93
Eastbourne – Beachy Head 93

James Bond in Essex 97
Stansted Mountfitchet – Stansted Airport 97
Southend-on-Sea – London Southend Airport 100

James Bond in Hampshire 105
Aldershot – Bruneval Barracks, Eelmoor Driver Training Area 105
Camberley – Minley Training Area 108
Farnborough – Farnborough Airport 109

5

Contents

Odiham – R.A.F. Odiham 111
Southampton – Southampton Docks 113
   Miscellaneous Locations **116**
      Beaulieu – National Motor Museum 116
      Lee-on-the-Solent – The Hovercraft Museum 120
      Portsmouth – Portsmouth Naval Base 122

James Bond in Hertfordshire **125**
Abbots Langley – Leavesden Studios 125
Bovingdon – Bovingdon Airfield 126

James Bond in Kent **129**
Chatham – The Historic Dockyard Chatham 129
Dover – Port of Dover Ferry Terminal 131
Manston – Kent International Airport 134

James Bond in Norfolk **137**
Burnham Deepdale – Deepdale Farm 137
   Miscellaneous Location **139**
      Snetterton – Snetterton Park Models 139

James Bond in Northamptonshire **141**
Silverstone – Silverstone Circuit 141

James Bond in Oxfordshire **143**
Chinnor – Chalk Quarries 143
Finmere – Finmere Airport 145
Oxford – Brasenose College, New College 146
Stonor – Stonor Park, Whitepond Farm 151
Upper Heyford – R.A.F. Upper Heyford 155
   Miscellaneous Locations **164**
      Drayton St. Leonard – Aston Martin Heritage Trust 164
      Nettlebed – Joyce Grove 165

James Bond in Suffolk **169**
Eleveden – Eleveden Hall 169
Lakenheath – R.A.F. Lakenheath 171

James Bond in Surrey **175**
Cranleigh – Dunsfold Aerodrome 175
Elstead – Hankley Common 178
Epsom – Epsom Downs Racecourse 181
Stanwell – Esso West London Terminal 182

James Bond in West Sussex **185**
Amberley – Amberley Museum & Heritage Centre 185

Contents

James Bond in Wiltshire 191
Swindon – Spectrum Building, Vygon (ex Motorola) Building 191
   Miscellaneous Locations 194
     Highworth – The Goldfinger Tavern 194
     Sevenhampton – Sevenhampton Place, St. James' Church 195

James Bond in Scotland 197

James Bond in Argyll and Bute 199
Garelochhead – H.M. Naval Base Clyde 199
Kilmichael Glassary – Barrachuile 201
Loch Craignish – Lunga Pier, Crinan, Craobh Haven 204
   Miscellaneous Location 211
     Duntrune – Duntrune Castle 211

James Bond in Highland 213
Dornie – Eilean Donan Castle 213
Glencoe – Glen Etive 215
   Miscellaneous Location 219
     Dalness – Dalness Lodge 219

James Bond in Wales 221

James Bond in Cardiganshire 223
Penbryn – Penbryn Beach 223

James Bond in Gwynedd 225
Beddgelert – Cym Dyli Pipeline 225

James Bond on Location Maps 227

Places Index 235

Film Index 237

Acknowledgments 239

THE ENTIRE SERIES OF *JAMES BOND ON LOCATION* IS AVAILABLE FROM ALL GOOD BOOKSHOPS OR DIRECT FROM THE PUBLISHER

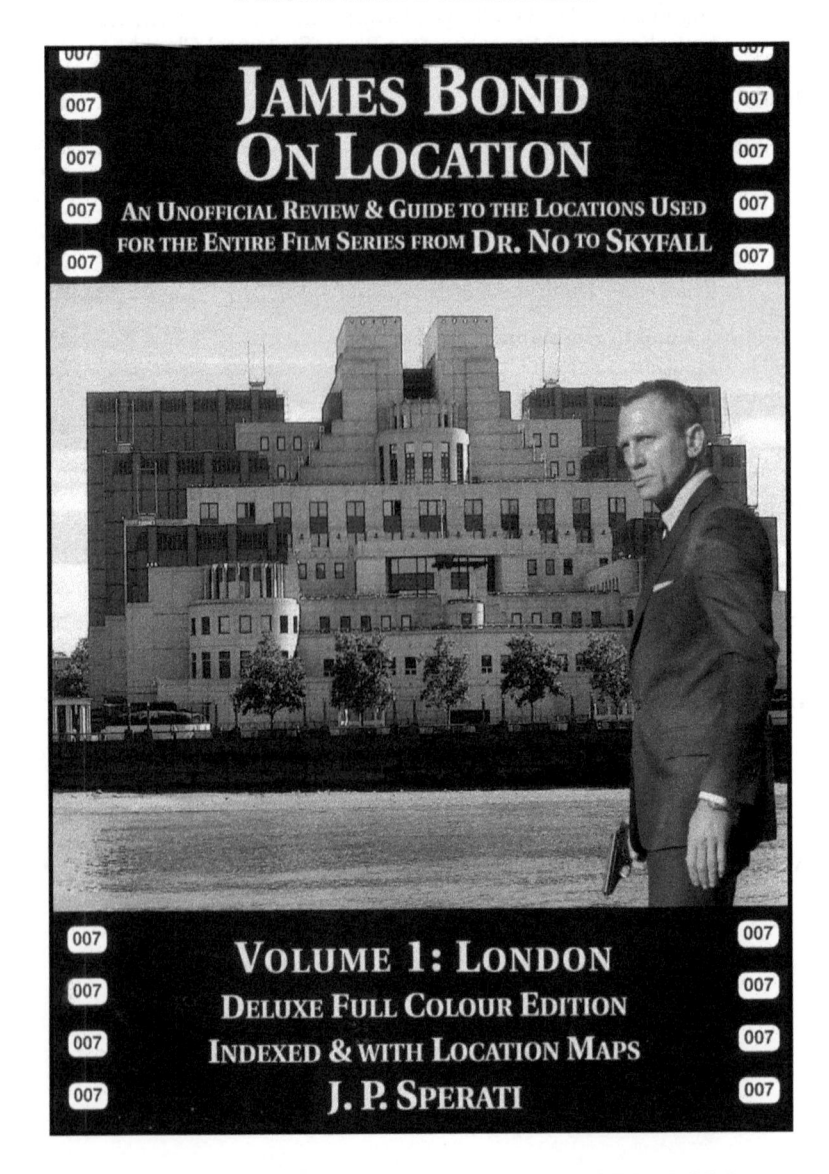

JAMES BOND ON LOCATION

An Unofficial Review & Guide to the Locations Used for the Entire Film Series from Dr. No to Skyfall

Volume 1: London

Deluxe Full Colour Edition

Indexed & with Location Maps

J. P. Sperati

WWW.JAMES-BOND-ON-LOCATION.COM
WWW.BAKER-STREET-STUDIOS.COM

INTRODUCTION

'The scent and smoke and sweat of a casino are nauseating at three in the morning.'

There is no conceivable way that Ian Fleming could have known that this first line, written on the 17th February 1952, in his first James Bond book, *Casino Royale*, would lead to his fictional spy being known the world over, and that it would culminate in the longest, and most successful, film franchise in history.

In this book Bond is cold and ruthless. He drives a 1933 4.5 litre Bentley, drinks champagne and dry Martinis (shaken, not stirred), smokes Morland cigarettes and carries a .25 Beretta automatic. Not exactly the iconic image portrayed on film although the basics are all present. To date the books (twelve novels and two collections of short stories) have sold in total around one hundred million copies – not bad for an author with a literary span of just over a decade, *Casino Royale* being published on the 13th April 1953 and his last book, *Octopussy and The Living Daylights*, just ninety-four pages in length, being released on the 23rd June 1966, nearly two years after Fleming's death on the 12th August 1964. For any normal author this would have been the extent of the canon, but not for Bond, since new stories have been written by the likes of Kingsley Amis (under the pseudonym of Robert Markham), Christopher Wood, John Gardner, Raymond Benson, Sebastian Faulks and Jeffery Deaver.

The books, though, may be considered small fry compared to the film success. To date there have been twenty-three 'official' films plus the satirical spoof version of *Casino Royale* and the 1983 remake of *Thunderball*, in which Sean Connery played Bond for the final time in the appropriately named *Never Say Never Again*. To complete the picture there was also a 1954 American television adaptation of *Casino Royale* called *Climax!*.

Total box office sales are estimated to be in the order of nearly S5 billion (or $12 billion if inflation is taken into account) on a total budget of around $1 billion (giving a healthy return on investment). It is thought that around one in five people on Earth have seen a James Bond film. Critically, however, the films have been less successful, having won just three Academy Awards in fifty-one years – for sound effects in *Goldfinger*, for visual effects in *Thunderball*, and most recently for best original song in *Skyfall*. 'Live and Let Die', 'Nobody Does It Better' (from *The Spy Who Loved Me*) and 'For Your Eyes Only' were all nominated in that category, but Adele's was the first Bond movie song to win.

Introduction

If one takes notice of the critics then the earlier films in the series are the best, with the three least satisfying being *You Only Live Twice*, *The Man With The Golden Gun* and *A View to a Kill*. A recent poll of over three thousand fans in 2012, prior to the release of *Skyfall*, concluded that the best film was *On Her Majesty's Secret Service*, closely followed by *Goldfinger* and *From Russia With Love* in that order. Looking at the highest ranking films portrayed by other actors, *The Living Daylights* came seventh, *The Spy Who Loved Me* eighth, *GoldenEye* ninth and *Casino Royale* fourth (not to be confused with the spoof version of the same title which came last). The worst 'official' Bond film was *Die Another Day*, which was not saved even by its $142 million budget.

The most successful, financially, at least, was *Dr. No* costing just $1.2 million and grossing nearly $60 million at the box office. George Lazenby was perhaps hard done by, since *On Her Majesty's Secret Service* had a reduced budget of $7.5 million, compared with $9.5 million for the previous film, *You Only Live Twice*, but still brought in a return of over ten fold. Likewise *Diamonds Are Forever* also had a small budget of just $7.2 million but recouped a sixteen-fold return, mainly due to the re-appearance of Sean Connery. The least successful film belongs to Roger Moore – *The Man with the Golden Gun*, which with its exotic locations cost $13 million to produce but grossed just under £100 million. The sales figures speak for themselves in that, although the critics may not be won over by James Bond, the rest of the world has always been in love with this film franchise. Indeed *Skyfall* has broken all previous United Kingdom box office records, being the first film of any kind to take more than £100 million at the box office, while in America it was the fourth highest grossing film of 2012.

But what is it about a Bond film that makes it such a success?

To some it is the story and script, while for many it is the actual portrayal of Bond, whether your favourite be Connery, Lazenby, Moore, Dalton, Brosnan or Craig. This is closely followed in popularity by the villains – who can forget the famous dialogue exchange with Goldfinger when Bond asks, "Do you expect me to talk?" to which the former replies, "No, Mr. Bond, I expect you to die!". Then there are the cameo appearances by M and Q, with his assortment of gadgets, that are almost expected in each outing, and of course a Bond film would simply not be a Bond film without those Bond girls, not forgetting their appearance in silhouette form in the stylish titles that were first inspired by Maurice Binder. Just as much a part of each film is the pre-title sequence, which sets the pace of each film, along with the gun barrel sequence. Let us not forget the stunts and action sequences, which most films cannot begin to match. Also central to each film is the music, which seems to fit seamlessly into each new adventure.

Introduction

Finally there are those exotic locations, and magnificent larger than life sets initially created by Ken Adam, as Bond goes around the world, and even into outer space if the end titles to *Moonraker* can be believed.

Hence the answer is not as simple as one might expect. To be successful, a Bond film may need only one or two of these elements, but most rely on a careful balance of them all. In just two words Bond can be considered as 'sheer escapism' for a couple of hours from the real dreary world that most of us inhabit.

It is to the last of the cited reasons, the locations, that this book is dedicated, and in this volume it is just the United Kingdom locations (excluding London which is covered in Volume 1 of this series) that are considered. At first this may not seem a good starting place, for Bond works for MI6, and therefore spends all of his time out of the country, except when he is being briefed by M in London at the start of an adventure.

Nothing could be further from the truth, for as Bond is a quintessentially British film production for the international market it follows that quite a lot of filming takes place in the United Kingdom. Just because in *Tomorrow Never Dies* the caption on the screen reads South China Sea, it does not necessarily mean that filming took place there, and indeed in this example it was RAF Lakenheath in Suffolk (page 171) that doubled for the more exotic location. In a similar manner, parts of Switzerland, India and Uganda can be found at Black Park in Buckinghamshire (page 31), Montenegro in Bedfordshire (page 17), France in Berkshire (page 26), East Germany in Cambridgeshire and Oxfordshire (pages 75 and 155 respectively), Iceland in Cornwall (page 89), Gibraltar in East Sussex (page 93), North Korea in Hampshire, Norfolk and Wales (pages 108, 137 and 223 respectively), Russia in Surrey (page 181), Morocco in Suffolk (page 169), with perhaps the most unlikely of all being when Swindon stood in for Turkey (page 191). It is amazing what a little set dressing can do to fool the viewer.

Even those places that are supposed to be in the United Kingdom can be deceptive, for Kent has stood in for central London (page 129), and Buckinghamshire for Scotland (page 69), while most recently in *Skyfall* Surrey has also stood in for Scotland (page 178).

Finding out just what was filmed where is all part of the fun of being a location detective, and if this aspect of filming interests you then read on, but beware, as certain myths about filming will be dispelled, and in future you will not be able to look at another Bond film without wondering

Introduction

whether what you see on the screen is actually where the filming took place, because much of the time it isn't.

I hope that you enjoy reading this book, and using it to visit some of the places listed, as much as I did researching and compiling it for you.

J. P. Sperati

James Bond in England

JAMES BOND IN BEDFORDSHIRE

LUTON - LUTON HOO

[Side terrace and gardens at Luton Hoo]

This country house on the outskirts of Luton is a Grade I listed building. Luton Hoo is not mentioned in the Domesday book, but a family called de Hoo occupied a manor house on the site for four centuries, until the death of Lord Thomas Hoo in 1455. Successive houses on the site seem to have changed hands several times until in 1762 the then owner, Francis Hearne, sold the estate for £94,700 to John Stuart, the 3rd Earl of Bute. Following an unhappy period as Prime Minister from 1762 to 1763, Bute decided to concentrate his energies on his Bedfordshire estate at Luton Hoo.

Stuart employed the neoclassical architect Robert Adam to design and build a magnificent house. However, this plan was never fully executed and much of the work was a remodelling of the older house. Dr. Samuel Johnson, who visited in 1781, is quoted as saying, 'This is one of the places I do not regret coming to see … in the house magnificence is not sacrificed to convenience, nor convenience to magnificence'. While Adam was working on the mansion the landscape gardener Capability Brown was enlarging and redesigning the park, some 1,200 acres. Brown dammed the River Lea to form two lakes, one of which is 60 acres in size. In turn Adam's completed mansion was transformed by the architect Robert Smirke in around 1830, following the occupation of Stuart's grandson, the 2nd Marquis of Bute, to its present form today, complete with a massive portico. Luton Hoo is neither Gothic nor strictly Greek revival style, but an unusual example of a classical style for domestic use.

In 1843 a devastating fire occurred and much of the house and its contents were destroyed. The burnt shell was sold in 1848 to John Leigh, a Liverpool solicitor and property speculator. He rebuilt the house in the style and manner of Smirke, with his family living there until 1903, when the estate was sold to the diamond magnate, Sir Julius Wernher. (In 1863, during Leigh's residence, excavations on the estate uncovered nearly a thousand Roman coins from the third century AD.) Wernher had the interior remodelled by Charles Mewes and Arthur Davis, the architects of the Ritz Hotel in London. It was done in the *belle époque* style resulting in a magnificent backdrop for Wernher's acclaimed art collection. The marble-walled dining room was designed to display Beauvais tapestries, while the newly installed curved marble staircase surrounded Bergonzoli's statue *The Love of Angels*. At the centre of the house the massive Blue Hall displayed further tapestries, King Louis XV furniture, and Sèvres porcelain. Wernher's great art collection, equal to that of his neighbours in nearby Buckinghamshire, the Rothschilds, was later further enhanced by the marriage of Julius Wernher's son Harold Augustus Wernher to Anastasia Romanov, a member of the former Russian Imperial family, generally known as Lady Zia. She brought to the collection an incomparable assembly of renaissance enamels and Russian artefacts, including works by the Russian Imperial court jeweller Peter Carl Fabergé. For many years the collection and house were open to the public. However, many of the Fabergé items were stolen in the 1990s.

Following Lady Zia's death in 1977, the estate passed to her grandson Nicholas Harold Phillips, whose untimely death in 1991 caused its sale. The priceless collection is now on permanent display at Ranger's House in London. On 1st October 2007 the house entered a new era when it opened as a one hundred and forty-four bedroom luxury hotel, spa and golf course. Luton Hoo has appeared in many films including *A Shot in the Dark* (1964), *Four Weddings and a Funeral* (1994), *Eyes Wide Shut* (1999), *Wilde* (1997) and *Enigma* (2001). For the James Bond fan it has made two appearances. In *Never Say Never Again* it became Shrublands health farm, the outside being clearly recognisable as Bond arrives by car. More recently in 1999 the interior was filmed to double for Elektra King's residence in Baku in *The World Is Not Enough*. Athough the staircase and hall are again clearly recognisable, the bedroom scenes were in fact a studio set.

MILLBROOK - MILLBROOK PROVING GROUND

[The hills of Montenegro are actually here at Millbrook near Luton]

Millbrook takes its name from the nearby village where, in the early 19th century, a flourishing community of mills nestled around a picturesque brook. By the late 1800s the population exceeded six hundred but with the last of the mills being demolished by 1940 it rapidly declined to around one hundred and forty inhabitants today.

In 1923, the General Motors Technical Committee, under the chairmanship of Alfred P. Sloan Jr, decided, following a rather less than satisfactory brake test on public roads, that a road test surface should be built for future testing of vehicles. As a result work started on the General Motors Proving Ground at Milford, Michigan the following year. By 1963 the site comprised level sections, hills of various gradients and a high-speed banked oval track some 4.5 miles in circumference.

Meanwhile over in Britain in the mid 1960s, Vauxhall and Bedford decided that, whilst the new and almost deserted M1 motorway close to Luton presented some very interesting testing opportunities, a better policy for future vehicle development was to learn from the American experience and build a dedicated proving ground. The site chosen was Millbrook, which was to replicate many of the most successful features at Milford.

Construction began in April 1968 with over two and a half million cubic yards of earth being moved to sculpt the necessary track features into the existing landscape. At the height of the earth-moving work over fifty machines were employed, with three and a half thousand tons of hand-laid granite blocks forming the almost mile-long Belgian Pavé circuit, while seventy-three thousand tons of aggregate and nine thousand tons of cement went into the five lane high-speed circuit. The circular steering pad required six thousand cubic yards of hardcore, one thousand three hundred tons of cement and six thousand tons of aggregate. In addition over two hundred thousand trees were planted, both conifers and indigenous deciduous varieties, helping nature to return to an area that for many years had been notably lacking in natural beauty.

Initially only Vauxhall cars, Bedford trucks, buses and military vehicles used the site, but in 1988 Millbrook Proving Ground Limited became a subsidiary of Group Lotus. This was not to last as in 1993 Millbrook was separated from Group Lotus by transferring its shares to GM Holdings UK Limited. The company continued to flourish as an independently managed business, focussing investment on increasingly high technology areas of vehicle design, such as crash mitigation, emissions control and component durability. The core track-based whole vehicle durability business was also supported with new facilities and steady, profitable growth ensued. Today Millbrook has a worldwide client base and is one of Europe's leading locations for the development and demonstration of every type of land vehicle, from motorcycles and passenger cars to heavy commercial, military and off-road vehicles. The custom-built facility provides virtually every test and validation needed in today's demanding programmes, complemented by a worldwide reputation for confidentiality, service and competitiveness. In addition Millbrook engineer, develop and build low-volume service vehicles, trial and evaluate vehicle capability, investigate in-service failures and provide specialist driver training.

The *Casino Royale* production crew (over one hundred and fifty persons) visited Millbrook for five nights of location work, filming the dramatic car chase sequence in which Bond has to swerve in order not to hit Vesper Lynd, who has been bound and laid in the middle of the road by Le Chiffre. As a result Bond's Aston Martin flips in mid-air and rolls over no less than seven-and-three-quarter turns, a stunt that was entered into the 2006 edition of the *Guinness World Records*.

In fact stunt co-ordinator Gary Powell used three cars for the sequence. The Aston Martin used was the DBS model (not yet available to the public) which has an engine capacity of 5935cc and a top speed of nearly two hundred miles an hour. It was designed to be midway between the DB9 road car and DBR9 race car, and as a consequence has a deeper front spoiler, an extra-wide intake and a larger rear spoiler than the road car. These racing specifications meant that a standard ramp would not be sufficient to roll the car and as a result an air-powered cannon just behind the driver's seat had to be installed. This, when activated, pushes a metal cylinder into the road in order to flip the vehicle, and indeed if you look closely at the sequence you can see the cylinder on the underside as the car rolls. Adam Kirley was the person at the wheel for this spectacular stunt, which needed to be performed at eighty miles an hour.

[One of the Aston Martin DBS cars used for filming *Casino Royale*]

Please note that the Millbrook Proving Ground is a high security private commercial site not open to the public.

JAMES BOND IN BERKSHIRE
ASCOT - ASCOT RACECOURSE

[The current Ascot stand dating to 2006]

Ascot itself is just a small town of around eleven thousand people, with the central area comprising, in the main, fairly nondescript post-war buildings, although the town is also the unlikely home of the Chartered Institute of Building. It is within commuting distance of both London and Reading, and is served by frequent trains to both. Notable local residents have included John Lennon, Ringo Star and Marti Pellow.

However, by far the most important feature of Ascot is the racecourse, employing around seventy full time staff, which during Royal Ascot week in June rises to around six thousand persons. Royal Ascot is probably the most famous race meeting in the world, dating back to 1711, and sees the royal family attending, arriving each day in a horse-drawn carriage. The first ever race here was for Her Majesty's Plate, with a purse of one hundred guineas, on the 11th August 1711, with the royal person in question being Queen Anne, who founded the racecourse.

Today in order to gain access to the Royal Enclosure during Royal Ascot week one has to apply for tickets and gain membership from somebody who has attended the enclosure for at least four years, somebody such as Sit Godfrey Tibbett in *A View to a Kill*. The dress code is strictly enforced, with men needing black or grey morning dress complete with top hat, and women a day dress (of acceptable length and style) with a suitable hat. This is why M tells Bond that he has "exactly thirty-five minutes to get properly dressed". Some three hundred thousand people make the annual visit here, there being somewhere in the order of £3 million prize money on offer. This was of course one of the settings in *My Fair Lady* and the subject of the song 'Ascot Gavotte'.

In 1813 parliament passed an act to ensure that the ground would always remain a public racecourse, and to this day the public have free access to the area via a tunnel from the main road. A further act was passed in 1913 creating a body known as the Ascot Authority which has managed the racecourse ever since. Until 1945 the only racing that took place here was the four-day Royal Meeting. Further meetings have been added over the years, including steeplechases and hurdles from 1965, so that presently there are around twenty-six days of flat, and five days of National Hunt racing a year.

The racecourse closed for twenty months in 2004 for a £185 million redevelopment. As owner of the Ascot Estate, the Queen reopened the racecourse on the 20th June 2006. However, not everybody embraced the new grandstand design, complaining that it devoted too much space to restaurants and corporate entertainment at the expense of providing enough raised viewing for patrons. A further £10 million programme of improvements were undertaken to improve the viewing from the lower levels.

James Bond in Berkshire

[The Owners and Trainers Viewing Area just below the Royal Box]

The new grandstand does unfortunately mean that little remains of the filming location for *A View to a Kill* in which Bond observes Zorin and May Day for the first time, in the viewing area reserved for owners and trainers located just beneath the Royal Box.

To the rear of the grandstand is the Winners' Enclosure, and also a most remarkable sculpture entitled *Uniting Two Societies*. It comprises the original Harland and Wolf gates made prior to World War II through which the working class employees would pass. The associated sculptures include labourers, store men, carpenters, shipwrights, fitters, riveters, welders and riggers. The gates were damaged by enemy action during the war, and some of the damage has deliberately been left unrepaired. Also part of the scene are the Royal Ascot gates, through which many monarchs, royalty, prime ministers, presidents, world leaders, soldiers, sailors, airmen and numerous others, including owners, trainers and famous racehorses have passed. Some of these also appear in sculpture form. Hence in its entirety the sculpture portrays two levels of society, the establishment and the working class, coming together and meeting the Queen and Prince Philip at Royal Ascot.

[The Winners' Enclosure close to where May Day has trouble with Pegasus in *A View to a Kill*]

It is the Winners' Enclosure, though, that features in *A View to a Kill*, where May Day has trouble controlling Zorin's horse, Pegasus, who has just won a race and is suspected by Bond of having chemical help to do so.

Most recently the grandstand appeared fleetingly, doubling as Shanghai's Pudong International Airport, in *Skyfall*, as Bond is following the professional assassin, Patrice, to a city centre skyscraper where he is to perform another hit. Interestingly Epsom Downs racecourse doubled as St. Petersburg Airport in *GoldenEye* (page 181) though few people probably ever notice when visiting either racecourse that its architecture is similar to that of many modern airports.

HURLEY - HURLEY LOCK

Located on the banks of the River Thames between Marlow and Henley-on-Thames, the village of Hurley dates from Saxon times and was originally home to a Benedictine priory founded in 1086. Although the priory was dissolved by King Henry VIII, the priory church still survives as the local parish church of St. Mary's, while the main building became Lady Place, the home of the Barons Lovelace, until it was demolished in 1837. As with most priories there was also a hostelry associated with it, in this case The Olde Bell, which claims to be the oldest still-working inn in Britain, with parts dating back to 1135. Hurley also has a manor house, Hall Place, dating back to 1728, which is now the home of the Berkshire College of Agriculture. The only famous, or more correctly infamous, resident of the village was a boy from Lady Place who claimed that his father had started the Great Fire of London in 1666 by throwing fire-bombs into the baker's shop in Pudding Lane. He was subsequently put on trial but not convicted since it was generally thought that he was lying.

["Great sport this punting". The approximate spot where Bond entertains Sylvia Trench in *From Russia with Love*]

This is one of the most picturesque parts of the Thames, and the lock at Hurley is unique, as the river divides here into several channels. In the past these were difficult to navigate due to their shallows and bends, and were made even worse by the local mills who built dams of timber and rubble to provide themselves with power. At first barges passed through flash locks, which was a hazardous process where a section of the weir was removed after which the barges were winched up or down on the strong current flowing through the breach. It was only in the 18th century that a safer passage was provided through a pound lock. Today the river is just as beautiful, and much cleaner as well, with salmon now a common sight as there is a salmon ladder at Hurley Weir. The Thames Path National Trail passes through Hurley. Downstream, in the village of Temple, walkers heading towards Marlow must cross to the south bank by the attractive Temple Footbridge. In the opposite direction are Frogmill, Hambleden Mill, Medmenham Abbey (notorious in the 1750s as the home of the Hell Fire Club) and Henley-on-Thames.

It was no doubt the scenery, as well as the quiet location, that tempted Bond to bring Sylvia Trench here in *From Russia with Love*. They evidently arrived in Bond's personal Mark IV drophead coupé (circa 1936) Derby Green Bentley, which we see parked just a few paces from where Bond and Sylvia are relaxing in a punt. Their idyll is soon interrupted, however, when Bond receives a message on his 'cricket' pager, instructing him to call the office. He does so on the car's MTS radio telephone, which at the time of filming in 1963 had only just been introduced in Britain. This unfortunately puts an end to Bond "reviewing an old case" as he tells Moneypenny. The actual location used for filming is still instantly recognisable just to the east of the lock.

WRAYSBURY - WRAYSBURY LAKE

Formerly part of Buckinghamshire until 1974 the village of Wraysbury, originally written as Wirecesberie in the Domesday Book, is in the very eastern part of the county, just twenty-two miles from central London. There is archaeological evidence to suggest that there was a Neolithic settlement here, many hundreds of flint tools from that period having been found close to where the parish church of Saint Andrew's now stands

The lands around Wraysbury were held by a number of noblemen, and the Manor of Wraysbury, comprising two thousand four hundred acres, and valued at £20, was first given by William the Conqueror to Robert Gernon, while in the time of King Henry I the village was a portion of the hunting grounds of nearby Windsor. Within the parish is Magna Carta Island where the Magna Carta was sealed in 1215 by King John. In the document it is Runnymede that is mentioned but it is widely held by historians that King John and his entourage were on the opposite bank of the River Thames in Wraysbury.

It was only in 1627 that the place ceased to be a Crown Manor when King Charles I, ever in need of money, sold the estate to a London merchant named John Sharowe for just over £800. The village population remained fairly static during the 19th century at around six hundred persons, most of who were involved with agricultural and mill work. There was a boost when the railway arrived in 1848 and today the village has a population of around four thousand, many of them being either commuters or workers at Heathrow Airport. From the 1930s a new industry developed due to the presence of large quantities of gravel, which was easily excavated and transported by lorry, with a considerable amount being used for the building of the nearby M25 motorway in the 1980s. The exhausted gravel pits have now become beautiful lakes and places where all manner of wildlife flourishes.

[The spot where in *A View to a Kill* the Rolls-Royce containing Bond and Tibbett is pushed by May Day into the lake]

One of the larger lakes is now used by the Wraysbury Lake Sailing Club, founded in 1956. It was here, just off Welley Road on the track leading to the club, that a key scene in *A View to a Kill* was filmed. An unconscious Bond, along with the body of the recently murdered Sir Geoffrey Tibbett, played by Patrick Macnee, is in the back of a Rolls-Royce Silver Cloud II, which we see driving along the road and stopping beside the lake. Zorin and May Day get out, and the latter then pushes the car into the water – but Bond, of course, escapes, by opening the door and breathing air from the car's tyres until the two villains have departed. The action supposedly takes place in France, but if you visit Wraysbury today you can identify the scene without much difficulty. The cement works in the background has gone, but the two islands are easily recognisable.

[Cubby Broccoli's Rolls-Royce Silver Cloud II from *A View to a Kill*]

In fact the car seen for most of the film is Cubby Broccoli's own Rolls-Royce minus his personalised number plate, CUB 1. His model had a 6.2 litre V8 engine, but when it came to the submersion scene the production company used an engine-less replacement. Although May Day was certainly athletic a heavy cable was actually used to pull the car in and out of the water.

JAMES BOND IN BUCKINGHAMSHIRE

BEACONSFIELD - ROYAL SARACEN'S HEAD HOTEL

[The view along London End, almost unchanged since filming in 1965, where Major Derval's car is seen approaching his hotel]

Beaconsfield is actually a corruption of Bekensfield, meaning a 'clearing in the Beeches'. Being conveniently situated close to the M40 motorway and having a mainline railway service to London as well, the area has become a sought-after place to live, and with so many fascinating buildings and history is also a great favourite with film crews. Like nearby Amersham it is split up into two parts, the Old Town and the New Town.

Walking through the Old Town feels like stepping back in time. With so many listed buildings, it is almost completely unspoilt. Its situation midway between London and Oxford made the Old Town an ideal stopping place *en-route* for horse-drawn coaches. There are still many signs of these enchanting old coaching inns and hostelries to be found today. Interestingly, it consists of four sections of road known as 'ends' – Aylesbury End, London End, Windsor End and Wycombe End – it is where the coach routes from these destinations met.

Benjamin Disraeli was the First Earl of Beaconsfield, and one of the town's famous residents was the children's novelist Enid Blyton. She lived at a house named Green Hedges from 1938 until her death in 1968. Unfortunately the house has been demolished to make way for newer properties. However, you are able to see a detailed miniature version at the Bekonscot model village. Reputed to be the oldest model village in the world, it is situated in the heart of the New Town. The whole of this fascinating attraction is set in the 1930s. Children and adults alike can enjoy and discover the secrets of the miniature landscape of villages, buildings, farms, castles, churches, woods, fields and countryside. There is also a miniature model railway running throughout the entire attraction along with a short narrow gauge railway on which visitors may ride.

[The Royal Saracen's Head Hotel from Windsor End]

The hotel on the corner of London End and Windsor End is the Royal Saracen's Head. It served as the exterior of the hotel where Major Derval was staying, and where he was replaced by a look-alike, in *Thunderball*. First the car sent from the air base to collect him is seen coming up London End and turning into the hotel inner courtyard (an opening that today is blocked off and is actually the hotel main entrance).

The car's arrival is watched by Count Lippe from a telephone box outside the hotel. (Originally on the corner, it has been moved a few yards along Windsor End.) Lippe calls Fiona Volpe, who is with Major Derval in his room, to warn her that the car has arrived. A few seconds later Derval's phone rings again; this time it is the hotel reception, to say that his car is waiting for him. While Derval is dressing, helped by Volpe, there is a knock at the bedroom door. He opens it – and comes face to face with his own double (Angelo Palazzi), who shoots him with a gas dart. The switch is made with the double going off to the air base, while the real Major Derval is bandaged up and returned by ambulance to Shrublands health farm where his arrival is to be observed by a suspicious Bond.

BLACK PARK

[The magnificent lake at Black Park, but beware of crocodiles!]

Black Park is a country park in Wexham, between Slough and Iver Heath, which rather conveniently backs onto Pinewood Studios (page 45), and there is even a private gate to allow unhindered access for film crews. Managed by Buckinghamshire County Council, it covers over five hundred acres of woodland, heathland, grassland and a large lake (covering fourteen acres), with some areas being designated as Sites of Special Scientific Interest. The park is actually part of the historic Langley Estate. First mentioned in 1202 it has belonged variously to Henry VIII, Princess Elizabeth and the 3rd and 4th Dukes of Marlborough. The lake contains carp, bream, pike, perch and roach, while on the surface visitors can see swans, grebes, coots and moorhens. There are around thirteen miles of footpaths, cycle paths, majestic pinetree-lined avenues (which lend their name to the adjacent film studios) all of which are accessible to the public every day of the year between 8 a.m. and dusk.

It should come as no surprise, then, that the park continues to be used by many film and television companies. In the past the woods and lake featured prominently in the Hammer Horror films from the late 1950s to the 1970s. In these films the location was often used to represent Transylvania. Five Carry On films, Monty Python's *And Now For Something Completely Different* (1971), *Atonement* (2007), *A Challenge for Robin Hood* (1967), *Wombling Free* (1977), *Batman* (1989), *Scrooge* (1970), *Stardust* (2007), *Treasure Island* (1950), *Willow* (1988), *The Wolfman* (2010), *The Charge of the Light Brigade* (1968), *Eden Lake* (2008), *Fahrenheit 451* (1966), *Johnny English* (2003) where the park café was used, *Superman II* (1980), *Supergirl* (1984), *Agent Cody Banks* (2003), *Sleepy Hollow* (1999), *Alice in Wonderland* (2010) and no fewer than five of the Harry Potter films are amongst many other productions that have all been filmed here.

On the small screen the location was used in *Regan* (the pilot of *The Sweeney*), *The Sweeney* (three episodes), *The Professionals* (two episodes) *Blake's 7* (where it appears as various different planets in three episodes), *UFO* (five episodes), *Film Fever*, *Doctor Who* (two episodes), *New Tricks* and *Waking the Dead* (in which a car was driven into the lake and later recovered).

The park has also been used four times in the James Bond films. It first became Switzerland for part of the famous Aston Martin DB5 car chase scene in *Goldfinger* as James Bond tries unsuccessfully to evade Oddjob. It appeared again in *Octopussy* as India, with James Bond emerging from the lake in a crocodile camouflage. In *The World is Not Enough* Black Park's versatility was again illustrated when it doubled for Azerbaijan, where tree felling from specially equipped helicopters was very much in evidence, and most recently was a substitute for Uganda and the meeting between Le Chiffre and Obanno (the leader of a guerrilla group) in *Casino Royale*.

In fact during an average year there are around two hundred days that the park is rented out for filming, bringing much needed income to the authorities, who charge anywhere between £2,500 and £4,000 a day. However, a filming day also includes the time to set up a production as well as clearing the site after filming. For example, in *Harry Potter and the Order of the Phoenix* the production crew actually inhabited the park for the best part of three months constructing a railway line and station, although the scenes involving the Hogwart's Express lasted on screen for less than two minutes and were filmed over just five days.

If you proceed from the café and information centre along the east side of the lake, this is where scenes from *The Lost Prince* (2003), *Wolfman* (2010), *First Knight* (1995), *Robin Hood* (2010), *Son of Rambow* (2007) and the Lumberjack's song from *And Now For Something Completely Different* (1971) were all filmed.

[Rather a tight fit for James Bond]

This is also where Roger Moore was filmed in his crocodile camouflage in *Octopussy*. It should be noted that the lake is equally at home substituting for a river, and has been the River Thames more than once in its film career. Continuing on from the top of the lake, you will soon come to a clearing where parts of *Henry VIII* (2003) with Ray Winstone, *The Mummy Returns* (2001), *Midsomer Murders* where a body is found on Whiteoaks golf course in the 2009 episode entitled *The Dogleg Murders*, and scenes of Hagrid's hut in the first two Harry Potter films were all shot.

[The former site of a Ugandan terrorist camp in *Casino Royale*]

It is also the scene of the Ugandan terrorist camp in *Casino Royale* where Le Chiffre, a private banker to terrorist groups around the world, is found. The broker for the deal is a Mr. White, who invests their money and manipulates stocks so they get a 100% return on the investment. The terrorists, lead by a man named Obanno, agree to allow the money to be taken for Le Chiffre's nefarious purposes.

[This became Baku in *The World Is Not Enough*]

Not much further along the main path from here you will come to a junction, at which you should turn right and follow the line of trees to a crossroads. Here you would appear to be in the middle of a forest, with a wide track in every direction cutting through dense pine woods. This is where the helicopter tree-felling scene in *The World is Not Enough* and many of the Hammer Horror and Carry On films were shot.

[Where Oddjob dispatches Tilly Masterson with his hat]

From here you need to turn right (i.e. south) and follow the main path back towards the lake. In fact you are now walking parallel to the path you took from the visitor centre, and will presently come across a clearing of great film significance. Not only was this the site for part of the alpine car chase in *Goldfinger* and the location of Fort Knox in the same film, but it is also where one might find giant spiders, hippogriffs, unicorns, dragons in cages and the odd basilisk, as four of the Harry Potter films also shared this location. As far as *Goldfinger* is concerned, from the time Bond discovers Tilly Masterson in the bracken, staking out Goldfinger's factory, until her death at the hands of Oddjob, the filming was nearly all done at Black Park.

BURNHAM BEECHES

[Beware of dangerous driving and oil slicks along this road!]

Burnham Beeches, just twenty-five miles west of London, was saved from development by the Kyrle Society. It has been managed by the City of London Corporation since they purchased it in 1879 and is still funded almost exclusively through the City's private funds. Burnham Beeches is open every day from 8 a.m. until dusk and attracts around half a million visitors a year, especially in the autumn when they come to admire the changing colours. It is first mentioned in the Domesday Book as being 'woodland enough to feed six hundred swine'. Today the site consists of woodland, heath, valley mire, coppice, ponds, streams and grassland, and is a conservation area for birds, bats and fungi as well as spot pigs, sheep, cows and ponies which have been re-introduced to the site.

The largely beech and oak woodland of over five hundred acres has been regularly pollarded (cutting a tree at head height, forcing it to send up new multiple shoots), with many trees estimated to be around four hundred and fifty years old. Their age, and the amount of deadwood in and around them, means that the woodland is rich in wildlife. More than sixty of the species of plants and animals here are either rare or under threat nationally. The area is protected as a National Nature Reserve, Site of Special Scientific Interest and a candidate Special Area of Conservation.

James Bond in Buckinghamshire

Sevenways Plain hill fort in the southwest part of Burnham Beeches is a rare example of a single rampart earthwork, used either as a stock enclosure or possibly a place of refuge. It comprises a range of earthworks that have been dated to the Late Bronze Age and Early Iron Age.

The close proximity of Pinewood (page 45), Shepperton and Bray film studios, and the outstanding natural beauty of Burnham Beeches have made it a desirable filming location. However, filming is tightly controlled due to recognition of the international importance for wildlife, and restricted to no more than twenty days per year, and then only at certain times, with filming in environmentally sensitive areas banned altogether. Revenue from filming goes directly to fund the upkeep and management of Burnham Beeches.

Since 1946 there have been over seventy-five different productions that have used Burnham Beeches as a location. Perhaps the most notable on the big screen are *The Crying Game* (1992), *First Knight* (1995), *Eden Lake* (2008), *King Arthur* (2004), *Robin Hood: Prince of Thieves* (1991), *The Princess Bride* (1987), *Who Dares Wins* (1982), *Time Bandits* (1981), *Agatha* (1979), *A Town Like Alice* (1956), *Great Expectations* (1946) and no fewer than three of the Harry Potter films.

On the small screen many classic television series have also made good use of the area, including *Dangerman, The Avengers, Z Cars, Manhunt, Randall & Hopkirk (Deceased), The Persuaders, The New Avengers, The Professionals* and *Minder*. More recently it may be familiar to those who watch *Kananagh QC, Merlin, Midsomer Murders, Waking the Dead, New Tricks, Primeval* and *Jonathan Creek*.

The James Bond enthusiast should head for Victory Cross and the car-free zone for this is where a small part of the alpine car chase in *Goldfinger* was filmed, including the sequence in which Bond dispatches a henchman's car utilising the oil slick option on his Aston Martin. Indeed, it is easy to distinguish which shots took place here, and those that were done at Black Park (page 31) since Burnham Beeches, as the name suggests, is a deciduous wood, whereas the latter consists almost entirely of pine trees.

It is worthy of note that once affected by the oil slick the henchman's car careers off the road and falls down a small cliff, ending up at Goldfinger's factory. This segment of the action took place at nearby Harefield (covered in Volume 1) and at Pinewood Studios (page 45) itself.

DENHAM - DENHAM QUARRY LAKES

[The former residence of Sir John Mills in Denham village]

The village name is Anglo-Saxon in origin, and means 'homestead in a valley'. It was listed in the Domesday Book of 1086 as Deneham. St. Mary's is the parish church and has a flint and stone Norman tower and Tudor monuments. The picturesque tree-lined High Street has no shops as one might expect, but does include several old red brick houses with giant wisterias. Because of its unspoilt charm the village has been used in countless film and television productions and has always attracted those associated with the industry. Among the notable personalities who have been residents in the village are Sir Roger Moore, Paul Daniels (magician), Shane Richie (actor), Jess Conrad (actor and singer), Robert Lindsay (actor), Raymond Baxter (television presenter) and Mike Oldfield (musician), while just up the road could be found Harry Saltzman and Cilla Black (singer). However, the most famous by far, and the only house to have a blue plaque outside, is the former home of the acting giant, Sir John Mills.

The area is best known to cinemagoers because of Denham Film Studios, founded in 1936 by Alexander Korda, which occupied nearly two hundred acres of land known as the Fishery, belonging to Lord Forres. With no fewer than seven sound stages, it was then the largest studio complex in

Britain. It boasted sophisticated lighting, a private water supply, departments for plumbing, woodwork, plastering, painting, electricians and make-up as well as the most modern processing laboratories (which included the establishment of Technicolor). So important were the studios that the Great Western Railway provided special fast trains from London direct to Denham.

Hungarian by birth, Korda became one of the most influential and flamboyant personalities in the British film industry, but unfortunately his magnificent vision was not supported by profits. The 1938 financial report by the studio backers, following large losses, stated that 'it is unfortunately true that on account of his temperament and opportunism in financial matters, Mr. Korda is a dangerous element in any business, more particularly if he is in a position of control', He was forced to relinquish control in favour of his chief rival, one J. Arthur Rank. Despite the financial problems, several fine films came out of Denham Studios, including *Things to Come* (1936), *Rembrandt* (1936), *The Thief of Bagdad* (1940), *In Which We Serve* (1942), *The Life and Death of Colonel Blimp* (1943), *Henry V* (1944) and *Brief Encounter* (1945). Denham's history as a major studio ended in 1952 with Walt Disney's *The Story of Robin Hood*, after which the complex served various commercial purposes before being demolished to make way for an industrial park.

[Denham Quarry Lakes, number three, as featured in *Thunderball*. The exact location used is hard to find after so may years but Volpe's motorcycle was pushed into the water somewhere along the far side of this picture, given that this is the only section of the entire area that has electricity pylons (clearly in view in the film) running parallel to the lake, although the water levels are now much higher than in 1965]

Just to the east of Denham is a series of lakes, that were formerly aggregate quarries providing raw materials for concrete production, but now flooded and used for more leisurely pursuits such as sailing and fishing. Since filming for *Thunderball* took place here in 1965 the area has matured, with the location where Fiona Volpe dumps her BSA motorcycle into the lakes, having just killed Count Lippe (page 141), being almost unrecognisable today. The actual location is what is known as lake number three with the Grand Union Canal and an electricity pylon (clearly in shot) in the background.

GERRARDS CROSS - CHALFONT PARK HOUSE

[Shrublands, just the place for Bond to rest in *Thunderball*]

Exclusive is a word often associated with Gerrards Cross, and due to its many celebrity residents it has also been referred to as 'mini Hollywood'. It is said that outside of London (Heathrow airport is just fourteen miles away) this is the most expensive postcode in which to buy property. Gerrards Cross is not an ancient village, having only come into existence in 1859 when it was formed by taking pieces of land from five parishes (Chalfont St. Peter, Fulmer, Iver, Langley Marish and Upton). It takes its name from the Gerrard family, who in the 17th century owned a manor here in what was then the hamlet of Chalfont St. Peter. Prior to that it was the site of an Iron Age hillfort.

The local church, dating from 1861, and dedicated to St. James, is of interest architecturally, having a Byzantine style dome, Chinese looking turrets and an Italianate campanile. In 1969 Lulu, the singer, married Maurice Gibb of the Bee Gees here, and Margaret Rutherford is buried in the graveyard.

Running parallel with the main A413 Amersham Road as it bypasses Gerrards Cross is Chalfont Park, and along here, just past the golf club, will be found Chalfont Park House, currently being used as offices for a software company. The building is little changed from the 1960s and should be instantly recognisable to the James Bond enthusiast as Shrublands, the health farm to which Bond is sent in *Thunderball*.

HALTON - HALTON HOUSE

[Halton House becomes a Baku casino in *The World Is Not Enough*]

Halton is a small village in the Vale of Aylesbury, about two miles from Wendover and five from Aylesbury itself. The Wendover arm of the Grand Union Canal flows through the village on its course from Wendover to Marsworth lock, near Tring.

The area is dominated by R.A.F. Halton, a training station with a grass airfield used for glider training. The base had a large military hospital employing thousands of people, which was closed in 1995. The buildings have since been demolished in favour of the Princess Mary Gate housing scheme.

In 1913 Alfred de Rothschild, who owned the Halton Estate, invited no. 3 Squadron of the Royal Flying Corps to use his land for summer manoeuvres, the first flight being recorded on the 18th September. At the outbreak of World War I Rothschild offered Lord Kitchener the use of the estate for the British Army, and by 1916 the area was covered in tents, with some twenty thousand troops under training. That same year the R.F.C. moved its air mechanics school from Farnborough to Halton, and in 1917 the school was permanently housed there in workshops constructed by German prisoners of war.

Alfred de Rothschild died in January 1918, and the War Office seized the opportunity to purchase the whole estate on behalf of the Royal Air Force, which would come into being in April of that year. The price paid was £112,000; clearly a bargain, for included in the sale was the family residence, Halton House (one of several houses owned by the Rothschilds), built in 1883 in a French style.

It had been the scene for Alfred's sparkling weekend house parties, which attracted the cream of British society. Today it is the Officers' Mess. In fact there had been a house on the site since the Norman Conquest, at which time it belonged to the Archbishop of Canterbury. In the mid-16th century Thomas Cranmer sold it to Henry Bradshaw, the Chancellor of the Exchequer. In 1720 it was in turn sold to Sir Francis Dashwood and in 1853 became the property of Lionel de Rothschild. However, the house became uninhabited and was in ruin when the estate, comprising some one-and-a-half thousand acres, was given to Alfred de Rothschild who demolished the house. The new building that sprang up in just three years is very much influenced by nearby Waddesdon Manor (page 72), the home of Baron Ferdinand de Rothschild, his brother-in-law. Although not as large it does have many of the same architectural features, such as classical pediments jutting out from mansard roofs, spires, gables and a giant cupola. In fact it was described as looking somewhat like a giant wedding cake. The inside was furnished in what is known as *le style Rothschild*, i.e. 18th century

French furniture, boulle, ebony, and ormolu, complemented by Old Masters and fine porcelain.

In 1919, Lord Trenchard established the No. 1 School of Technical Training at R.A.F. Halton, where it remained until 1993 when it was moved to R.A.F. Cosford. In addition, during World War II the base was host to 112 and 402 Squadrons of the Royal Canadian Air Force.

Today the establishment is the gateway to the Royal Air Force and, although it no longer trains aircraft engineers, it does provide nine weeks of basic training before recruits continue on their individual trade training. In October 1997, R.A.F. Halton was honoured with a Queen's Colour in recognition of its outstanding contribution to training over many years. The Trenchard Museum, which is dedicated to the history of the base, is open to the public on Tuesdays.

[The main gaming room in Valentine Zukovsky's Casino Noir d'Or]

Halton House has featured in a number of television and film productions including *Jeeves and Wooster*, *Evita* (1996), *An Ideal Husband* (1999), *What a Girl Wants* (2003), *The Queen* (2006), *Flyboys* (2006), *The King's Speech* (2010) and *Downton Abbey*. In *The World Is Not Enough* Halton House becomes the casino owned by Bond's old enemy, Valentine

Zukovsky, which Bond visits in an attempt to find out more about Renard and the men who attacked him earlier. This is also where Elektra makes an appearance to show that she isn't afraid of her enemies and in hope of winning a sizable amount of money using her father's standing credit. In the end she loses on a high-low draw of cards but is gracious in defeat.

IVER HEATH - PINEWOOD STUDIOS

[Is this the Pinewood mansion, or maybe a training camp on SPECTRE Island?]

The old mansion at the centre of the Pinewood Studios complex was originally a private residence, called Heatherden House, before being purchased by building tycoon Charles Boot and turned into an exclusive country club of some one hundred and fifty-six acres. Boot subsequently changed the club's name to Pinewood, due to 'the number of trees that grew there'. However, his ultimate plan was to turn the estate into a film studio. In 1935 he entered into a partnership with J. Arthur Rank, a devout Methodist who wanted to make films with a religious or strong moral theme. Work soon commenced on the new studio, with the old mansion being kept for administrative purposes. Their dreams were finally realised on 30th September 1936 when Pinewood Studios Limited were officially opened by the Parliamentary Secretary to the Board of Trade. The same year Herbert Wilcox bought his way onto the board with a 50% stake, using the insurance money from his own studios, the British and Dominions at Elstree, which had been destroyed by fire.

Forty-seven films had been made at Pinewood by the time war broke out in 1939, but the studios had actually closed the previous year, due to financial difficulties, and productions were transferred to Denham Studios, which by then were owned by J. Arthur Rank. Once war was declared the studios were requisitioned by the British government and served variously as offices for Lloyds of London, as a base for the Royal Air Force and Crown Films Unit, and as an out-station for the Royal Mint (with comments being made that this was the first time that Pinewood Studios were in the money!). The studios were re-opened in 1946 and managed another thirty-two productions by the end of the decade including *Kind Hearts and Coronets* (1949) which although billed as an Ealing Comedy was shot here. However, the company was still not profitable, in part due to the advent of television, and in part due to an embargo on British films being shown in the States, in retaliation to the British government's 75% tax on box office earnings on American films screened in the United Kingdom.

With the financial situation in mind, Pinewood Studios concentrated on films with popular appeal. They were successful too, with titles such as *Genevieve* (1953), *A Town Like Alice* (1956) and *Doctor in the House* (1954), that last spawning a whole series of comedies, as did *Carry On Sergeant* (1958). Just as things were looking up, the studios with great publicity announced that they were embarking on what became the most expensive non-event ever, *Cleopatra* (1963), starring Elizabeth Taylor, Richard Burton and Rex Harrison. Lavish sets were built, Elizabeth Taylor became seriously ill and needed a long period of convalescence, and the English weather did not help either. In the end the film was made in Italy leaving a large hole in the finances once again.

However, rescue was at hand in the form of two film producers, one Canadian and the other American – Harry Saltzman and Albert R. Broccoli respectively – who having formed EON Productions cast an unknown struggling actor called Sean Connery to play the role of James Bond in the first film of the series, *Doctor No* (1962). Other successes followed, with one hundred and sixty films being made at Pinewood Studios in the 1960s, along with a few television productions. The 1970s saw an increase in television productions and a decrease of films to one hundred and twenty-five productions. In 1976 the world's largest soundstage, the 007 Stage, was built on the backlot. Although fewer films were being made there, just two blockbusters such as *Superman: The Movie* (1978), which occupied all twenty stages, could put Pinewood Studios in profit for a whole year.

In April 1985 the British government phased out the capital tax allowance scheme which had encouraged British productions to be made in the United Kingdom. There was an immediate decline, with only fifty films being made at Pinewood Studios during the 1980s. In fact in 1987 Pinewood Studios became a 'four-waller', meaning that it was no longer a fully-serviced studio, but that producers could hire freelance outside labour for their productions.

Despite redundancies, it did attract many more productions in the 1990s, including work for television commercials, and overall increased profits to the extent that in 2000 the Rank Group plc sold Pinewood Studios for just over $99.2 million to a management buy-in team led by Michael Grade. Finally in 2001 Pinewood and Shepperton Studios merged to form a studio with joint facilities to match any Hollywood studio, and today the place is busier than ever, being known not only for its facilities but the technical expertise as well. The gardens around Heatherden Hall are another big attraction for film makers and have graced the screens in countless television series and films over the years. These formal gardens include a picturesque lake, fountain and bridge, making it an irresistible attraction for film crews.

Pinewood is one of Europe's leading film, television and media complexes. Recently plans have also been granted for the redevelopment of the existing studio site to improve the facilities. The vision is headlined as 'Project Pinewood, the first purpose-built living and working community for film, television and the creative industries'.

Some of the country's most famous films have used the facilities here. These include, *Slumdog Millionaire* (2008), *Mamma Mia* (2008), *The League of Extraordinary Gentlemen* (2003) and the aforementioned Carry On series, to name but a few. Television productions include *New Tricks*, *Jonathan Creek*, *Little Dorrit*, *The Avengers*, *UFO*, *Midsomer Murders* and the United Kingdom version of the quiz show, *The Weakest Link*, with host Anne Robinson.

Readers should remember that Pinewood Studios are not open to the public and employ state of the art security systems to keep film spotters away, so please under no circumstances visit expecting to gain entry. However, the studios also host conferences and the like, so it may be possible to get a chance to see behind the scenes of the screen home of James Bond, and the following are some things for which to keep a lookout.

Only two Bond films have not been shot at Pinewood. *Licence to Kill* used the Churubusco Studios in Mexico, mainly because the British government's abolition of the Eady Levy in 1985, resulting in foreign artists being taxed more heavily, made it more economical to film outside the U.K. When it came to the next film, *GoldenEye*, Pinewood was not available, and rather than delay filming by a year the producers chose to set up an entirely new studio at the old Rolls-Royce factory at Leavesden (page 125).

It should also be said that Pinewood was only used for model shots (of the cable car interiors and space battle exteriors) in *Moonraker*, since due to tax considerations it was an advantage to be based outside the United Kingdom (in France at Épinay and Boulogne-Billancourt Studios), while for *Tomorrow Never Dies* neither Pinewood or Leavesden (who were busy filming *Star Wars Episode I: The Phantom Menace*) could accommodate such a large production. The solution was once again to build a new studio, this time near St. Albans at what became known for a short time as the Frogmore Studios (which once filming was completed returned to being a derelict industrial site that has since been demolished). However, the scenes involving Carver's stealth ship were done at Pinewood. The same is true of *Casino Royale*, the main film studios used being the Barrandov Studios in Prague, with Pinewood only taking over for some minor scenes towards the very end of the film.

[The bridge from the opening shot of the pre-title sequence of *From Russia With Love*]

James Bond in Buckinghamshire

[The line of bushes where Red Grant stalks the Bond look-a-like ending up in front of the Pinewood mansion]

[The Bond look-alike pauses by the statue at the end of the path]

The SPECTRE training camp in *From Russia With Love* is in fact the Location Gardens at Pinewood. If you are lucky enough to visit the studio, you may be able to walk over the bridge, past the fountain, and along the line of trees, where the James Bond look-alike is followed and strangled by Red Grant in the film's pre-title sequence.

[The line of bushes and path is recognisable in *From Russia With Love*]

[Just the spot for a quiet massage on SPECTRE Island]

When the lights are turned on at the end of this scene and the supervisor says, "Exactly one minute, fifty-two seconds. That's excellent," the handsome building in the background is the famous Pinewood mansion (see photograph on page 45).

Later in the film Rosa Klebb arrives by helicopter to the side of the mansion, close to the gate (in shot) leading to the car park, easily identified since this part of the building is not painted in white, and proceeds to walk through the SPECTRE training area to meet Red Grant. The scene where Klebb punches Grant with her knuckle-duster and then proclaims that "he seems fit enough. Have him report to me in Istanbul in twenty-four hours", takes place beside the lake.

[The fountain the Bond look-a-like passes, along with some large trees in the background which feature in *Goldfinger*]

This part of the garden was also utilised in the next Bond film, *Goldfinger*, in which a helicopter is seen hovering over some large pine trees (mainly Black Park, page 31), searching for Bond and Pussy Galore, who have just parachuted from an aeroplane, having successfully disposed of Goldfinger. This is supposedly America as Bond is on the way to lunch with the president in the White House. Bond pulls the parachute over Pussy Galore, who is attempting to signal for help, and utters, probably the best closing line of the entire film series, saying, "Oh no you don't; this is no time to be rescued".

Earlier in the film the gardens are also the setting in which Oddjob, after the golf match between Bond and Goldfinger, is instructed to demonstrate his unique skill with his bowler hat. Although most of this sequence was done at Stoke Poges (page 66) the actual decapitation of the statue was at Pinewood, the statue being a prop with wires to achieve the required effect, and filmed at the side of the main house with the gate to the car park in view. This time it is Goldfinger who has the final quip in answer to Bond's question, "Remarkable, but what does the club secretary have to say?" as he answers, "Nothing. Mr. Bond. I own the club".

[The monument to Desmond Llewellyn who appeared as 'Q' in every Bond film, save *Live and Let Die*, between 1963 and 1999]

In fact the gardens are full of similar such statues and ornaments. Also to be found in the gardens, away from the house and lake, is a small grotto that has been used twice in the films. In *The World Is Not Enough* it is where Renard has a meeting with Elektra's head of security, while in the pre-title sequence of *Die Another Day* it is where Bond and his two colleagues change out of their surfing gear.

Finally, just over the other side of the bridge featured in *From Russia With Love* will be found a simple, but touching, piece of slate dedicated to 'Q'. This marks the contribution of actor Desmond Llewellyn, who played Q for thirty-six years to the James Bond films.

[The corner of Carpenters Road and Goldfinger Avenue close to Goldfinger's Swiss smelting operation]

The main complex consists of a number of stages, and other buildings, roughly arranged in a grid system. The roads between them are named in various ways from the unimaginative, Covered Way, Main Road, Studio Drive, Services Way and so on, to those with instant recognition such as Broccoli Road, Goldfinger Avenue and 007 Drive. Goldfinger Avenue is where Bond sees Auric Goldfinger's Rolls-Royce being dismantled and taken for smelting. Here too he first hears of Operation Grand Slam, a name that will save his life in due course. Almost immediately Bond is chased in his Aston Martin through these streets, doubling as part of Goldfinger's Swiss factory, having already used the car's ejector seat to dispose of one of Goldfinger's henchman. The chase ends when he mistakes the reflection of his own headlights for an oncoming vehicle and drives the car into a wall.

Apart from the gardens the largest area of open space at Pinewood is the Paddock Lot, which is sandwiched between the gardens and Black Park (page 31) to which there is a private gate. It is here that sets such as the gypsy camp in *From Russia With Love*, and the caviar factory in *The World Is Not Enough* were constructed. Butting onto the south side of the gardens is the smaller Back Lot where Goldfinger's stud, Blofeld's volcano in *You Only Live Twice*, the German town square in *Octopussy* and the demilitarised zone and ice palace in *Die Another Day* were all constructed. The only other open space for filming is the Cobbled Street area to the very north of the studios, and it was here that, for example, Fort Knox was built for *Goldfinger*.

[The Albert R. Broccoli 007 Stage with a London bus for size]

Next to the Pinewood mansion itself, the most famous building on site is undoubtedly the 007 Stage, built in 1976 for *The Spy Who Loved Me*. It is not only the largest building at Pinewood, but at the time was the largest silent sound stage in the world (and is still the largest in Europe), covering nearly five-and-a-half thousand square metres (with a tank of two thousand square metres).

The stage came about when Ken Adam was tasked to create the inside of the massive Liparus supertanker, which had to accommodate three submarines. It is said that Cubby Broccoli, in typical style, told Adam, "if you can't find a stage big enough to build your set in, why not construct a whole new one?". It was opened on the 5th December 1976 by the then former Prime Minister, Harold Wilson.

However, the stage does seem to have been jinxed, for on the 27th June 1984, at the end of filming *Legend* and just before shooting was to commence on *A View to a Kill*, the stage was burned to the ground. It was rebuilt in record time and was ready for filming in January 1985. There was a subtle change to the name as it now became the Albert R. Broccoli 007 Stage. It was burned down again on 30th July 2006, but this time just after the conclusion of filming for *Casino Royale*, while the Venetian piazza set was being dismantled. The current stage took just six months to construct and includes improvements such as increased working floor space, enclosed stairwells to the gantry, a vehicle ramp into the tank, aircraft style loading doors, increased electrical power and better insulation.

Since then it has been used by numerous productions to create amazing sets including the Channel Tunnel for *Mission Impossible* (1996), Cambodian Temples for *Lara Croft Tomb Raider* (2001), the Louvre Gallery for *The Da Vinci Code* (2006*)*, the Chocolate River Room for *Charlie and the Chocolate Factory* (2005) and the Greek fishing village in *Mamma Mia* (2008). As far as James Bond is concerned, apart from the aforementioned sets, the underwater wreck of the St. Georges in *For Your Eyes Only*, Kamal Khan's palace courtyard in *Octopussy*, Zorin's mine (which had to be flooded) in *A View to a Kill*, the Russian nuclear testing facility in *The World Is Not Enough*, the interior of the ice palace in *Die Another Day* and the Sienese art gallery and cisterns in *Quantum of Solace* were all constructed here.

The stage was also used for *Skyfall*. However, when the Bond production company moves in, it occupies more than a single stage. For *Skyfall*, for example, besides the 007 Stage, Stages A, B, C, D, F, G and S were all used, as well as the Exterior Tank and the Underwater Stage. As we have indicated, Pinewood only needs a couple of major productions to be in profit for the year.

MARLOW - THAMES LAWN

[The entrance to M's home through which Bond drives in *On Her Majesty's Secret Service*]

The attractive town of Marlow is situated on the River Thames, and its name derives from the Anglo-Saxon language, meaning 'land remaining after the draining of a pool'. It was recorded as Merelafan in the Domesday book.

All Saints Parish Church, with its tall steeple, sits majestically on the bank of the river, with the town's striking weir and lock just up-stream. This is undoubtedly one of the prettiest sights on the River Thames. Marlow, however, is doubly lucky in this respect: the present Marlow suspension bridge, built between 1829 and 1832, is also aesthetically very pleasing. It was designed by Tierney Clark, who also designed the Széchenyi Chain Bridge in Budapest (which was once the longest in the world). Plaques have been erected on the Marlow arches to commemorate the links between the two bridges.

James Bond in Buckinghamshire

The High Street has many old, interesting houses dating from the 16th, 17th and 18th centuries. Many of these have been sympathetically converted into shops. The renowned poet T. S. Elliot was once a resident in nearby No. 31 West Street from 1918-1919. Poet Percy Bysshe Shelley and his second wife Mary (author of *Frankenstein*) lived in the same street, albeit a century earlier, from 1817-1818. The Two Brewers public house in St. Peter Street, only a few minutes walk from the High Street, was established in 1755, and is rumoured to have been the inn where Jerome K. Jerome wrote some parts of his novel *Three Men in a Boat*.

Next door to The Two Brewers are the gates of Thames Lawn, the only feature still recognisable from the filming of *On Her Majesty's Secret Service* on the 9th April 1969. The aerial shot shows Bond driving through these gates and along the drive, past immaculate lawns, to the house by the river, where he is to report to M on his personal search for Blofeld. Sadly, nothing now remains of the original house, which was destroyed by fire in 1996 and has been replaced by a large modern mansion. There are also four flats, built in 1998 along Thames Lawn Mews, which now covers most of the gardens. In 2008, the lease on one of the flats was sold for more than a million pounds.

[How Thames Lawn looked at the time of filming]

The old house was actually a listed building, described in the documents as: 'Early C19. 2 storey. Painted stucco. Moulded cornice. Hipped slate roof. River front has flanking 2 storey wide angular bays, one wide double window between bays on 1st floor. Doric verandah of columns and entablature across ground floor. Projecting wing to right hand with one corner window. The west front of similar general design. A pleasant riverside house in large garden which forms an attractive end to the street'. After the fire, of course, the house was de-listed. Whether the new Thames Lawn will achieve the same recognition remains to be seen.

There is, however, still a plaque on the back wall to commemorate the fact that Vice Admiral Sir James Nicoll Morris, who was Captain of HMS Colossus at the Battle of Trafalgar, lived here between 1811 and 1830. It is entirely appropriate, then, that this should be chosen as M's home, given that Ian Fleming most likely based his character on Rear Admiral John Godfrey, who had been his superior at the Naval Intelligence Division.

NEWPORT PAGNELL - ASTON MARTIN WORKS

[The location of Q's workshop in *Diamonds Are Forever*]

Newport Pagnell, with a population in excess of fifteen thousand people, is generally regarded as being part of Milton Keynes, but is in fact a town in its own right and mentioned in the Domesday Book as Neuport, meaning a new market town. Pagnell refers to the Pagnell family who later came to own the manor. Originally the county assizes were held here, since the town was one of the largest in Buckinghamshire. The oldest cast iron bridge in the world is the famous one at Ironbridge in Shropshire, but the oldest such bridge still in constant use and carrying main road traffic is the Tickford Bridge in Newport Pagnell, built in 1810 to span the River Ouzel. For much of the 19th century the town had its own link to the Grand Union Canal in the aptly named Newport Pagnell Canal.

In Tickford Street itself a small factory opened in 1954 – this was the place where Aston Martin was to make its cars until 2007, when production was to move to a newer plant in Gaydon.

The company was founded in 1913 by Lionel Martin and Robert Bamford, who came up with the name of Aston Martin by combining Lionel Martin's name and that of the Aston Clinton Hillclimb where Martin used to race. The first Aston Martin, produced in 1915 at their premises at Henniker Place in Kensington (covered in Volume 1), had a four-cylinder Coventry-Simplex engine fitted to a 1908 Isotta-Fraschini chassis. World War I stopped any further production with both men seeing active service, and the machinery being sold to the Sopwith Aviation Company.

After the war the company was refounded, and in 1922 Bamford and Martin produced cars to compete in the French Grand Prix with world speed and endurance records being set at Brooklands the same year. Around fifty-five cars were built before the company went bankrupt in 1924. Lady Charnwood bought the company but it also failed in 1925, and the factory closed in 1926. Later the same year a group of investors resurrected the company at the old Whitehead Aircraft Limited works in Feltham and renamed it Aston Martin Motors.

Two of those investors were Bill Renwick and Augustus Bertelli, who were already in business producing engines with their own patented combustion chamber design. These they placed in a series of mainly open two-seater sports cars. The company saw financial trouble again in 1932, was again rescued, and in 1936 decided to concentrate on the production of road cars. By the outbreak of World War II, when the factory was turned over to producing aircraft components, a total of around seven hundred cars had been made.

In 1947 David Brown bought the company. He also acquired Lagonda and combined the company resources and workshops. From now on the cars were to bear his initials i.e. in 1950 the DB2 was announced, followed by the DB4 in 1958 and the DB5 in 1963. In 1955 David Brown bought the Tickford coachbuilding company in Newport Pagnell, which became known as the spiritual home of Aston Martin.

The cars appreciated in value and were much sought after, but the company itself was never stable. It suffered financial troubles in 1972, 1975 and much of the 1980s, until in 1987 the Ford Motor Company bought a stake in Aston Martin.

In 1994 a new factory was to open in Bloxham and the following year a record seven hundred vehicles came off the production line as the company moved away from hand coachbuilding methods. By 2002 the number of DB7s made had risen to six thousand. But even this did not help, for in 2007 the company was again sold after poor financial results, although Ford did still keep a stake in the new concern.

On the 19th July 2007 the very last Vanquish S rolled out of the Newport Pagnell factory. Around thirteen thousand cars had been built there since 1954. The site is still owned by Aston Martin and is today a dealership, restoration and service department.

The appeal of owning an Aston Martin has never been greater, and the company has expanded with more dealers in Europe as well as branches in China and the Far East. In 2008 it announced the revival of the Lagonda marque, but later the same year announced that a third of the workforce would have to be cut. However, the company still continues with the latest model, the Aston Martin Rapide, now being built at Gaydon.

The name of Aston Martin has of course become inextricably linked with that of James Bond, and the DB5 from *Goldfinger* is often cited as the most famous car in the world. It made a brief appearance the following year in *Thunderball*, and more recently, after flirtations with Lotus and BMW, has featured in *GoldenEye* (first seen parked in Oxford, where Bond is 'brushing up on a little Danish', and then back in London, driving through the entrance of MI6 [actually Somerset House – covered in Volume 1]), *The World Is Not Enough* (at the very end of the film in a satellite image, and in a deleted scene in which Bond arrives in the DB5 at the funeral of Robert King), *Casino Royale* (where we learn how Bond won the car from Alex Dimitrios in a poker game), and most recently in *Skyfall*.

Initially, in the books, at least, Bond drove a vintage four-litre Bentley, until in *Goldfinger* the head of Q Branch instructed him to take the Aston Martin DB III from the car pool. (In the books it's the department that is known as Q. Fleming named its head Major Boothroyd, after the firearms expert Geoffrey Boothroyd, who gave him much valuable advice, beginning with the suggestion that Bond's Beretta should be replaced with a Walther PPK.) The choice was dictated by the car's optional extras: reinforced bumpers, a gun underneath the driver's seat, a radio that could follow a tracking/homing device, and rear lights that could change type and colour. All rather tame compared to the ejector seat and other refinements seen in the film version, designed by Ken Adam and special effects man John Stears, who spent six weeks modifying the standard car supplied by Aston Martin.

After *Thunderball* in 1965 enthusiasts had to wait four years before an Aston Martin was to be seen again, now with George Lazenby as Bond in *On Her Majesty's Secret Service*. This time it was a new version of the DBS, based on a DB9 model, that Bond is seen driving at the very beginning of the film, as he saves Tracy Di Vicenzo from committing suicide in Portugal. Later he seen is in the car visiting M at his home in Marlow (page 56) and most memorably, at the very end of the film, it is in his DBS that Tracy is murdered on their wedding day, when Bond stops to remove the wedding flowers from the car.

Less obvious is the fact that in *Diamonds Are Forever*, when we see Q in his workshop, speaking on the telephone to Bond, he is actually in the Aston Martin paint shop at Newport Pagnell – which explains the DBS in the background.

[Timothy Dalton's V8 Volante complete with winter kit]

Timothy Dalton drives a modified Aston Martin V8 Volante in *The Living Daylights*. The vehicle used was actually that belonging to the then chairman of the company, Victor Gauntlett. It appears at the safe house (page 151), again in Q's workshop where it is being 'winterised' and of course in the chase scene filmed in Austria. For this exciting scequence, as Bond escapes through the Czech mountains to Austria with Kara Milovy, the cellist, two cars were used along with five other dummy cars.

Pierce Brosnan drove a V12 Vanquish, with adaptive camouflage, in *Die Another Day*. In fact seven cars were used for filming the ice chase scenes in Iceland, with two cars being written off. In *Casino Royale* the viewer having seen Bond in his DB5 early in the film, also gets to see him drive, and crash (page 17) a DBS. Finally, as if to out do former productions, no less than nine DBS's were used for the three-and-a-half minute car chase around Lake Garda at the opening of *Quantum of Solice*.

OAKLEY - R.A.F. OAKLEY

[The South American base blown up by Roger Moore in *Octopussy*]

Oakley is a village with just over a thousand inhabitants in Aylesbury Vale. The name in Old English simply means 'the clearing within the oaks'. Its most famous resident was Edward Brooks, a recipient of the Victoria Cross who was born here, but the area became infamous in 1963 when Leatherslade Farm, just outside the village, was found to be the hiding place for the gang known as the Great Train Robbers, who on the 8th August 1963 had held up a mail train at Bridego Bridge (some twenty-seven miles away) and stole £2.6 million, a record sum of money for the time, mainly in £1 and £5 notes. It was a local farmer, John Maris, who was the first to alert the police to the hiding place.

Between Oakley and Worminghall are the remains of the three-runway R.A.F. Oakley, built on requisitioned land at Field Farm in 1942. The base became operational in May 1942 and was always intended to be a satellite for nearby R.A.F. Westcott. However, R.A.F. Westcott had not been completed in time, and so the base was first designated as a second satellite for R.A.F. Bicester until the September, when it switched to its original purpose as an Operational Training Unit (mainly for air gunnery bomber crews for Wellington aircraft). Immediately after the war it became a base for the repatriation of prisoners of war (Operation Exodus) with over fifteen thousand men taking their first steps back in England at Oakley. Flying ceased in August 1945, and today only a B1 hangar and overgrown runways remain, most of the area having been returned to farmland.

Oakley was the name of the fictional air force base in England in the film *Pearl Harbor* (2001), although the filming was done at Badmington House in Gloucestershire. In 2003 the disused runway was featured in a *Midsomer Murders* episode (*A Talent for Life*) in which Honor Blackman drives along the runway at top speed in her red Jaguar sports car accompanied by her male friend. However, it is the remaining hangar that is of most interest to the James Bond enthusiast, since this is the hangar, supposedly in South America, that Bond flies through in his Acrostar jet (though most of this sequence was filmed at RAF Northolt, see Volume 1), and is subsequently destroyed (using some computer graphics), during the pre-title sequence of *Octopussy*.

Originally three Acrostars were purchased for filming in *Moonraker* but were never used. The BD-5J Microjet, as it is formally known, was invented by Jim Bede and at a weight of just four hundred and fifty pounds, and a wing span of thirteen feet is the lightest jet aircraft in the world. It has a top speed of three hundred and fifty miles an hour due to its powerful TRS-18 microturbo engine, which delivers two hundred and twenty-five pounds of thrust.

The hangar still remains and is in use today as the home of Natural Building Technologies, a company specialising in providing a number of environmentally sound structural building systems for walls, roofs and floors, as well as ranges of ecological paints, mineral plasters, renders and natural fibre insulation products.

[The Acrostar BD-5J Microjet with 'Little Nellie' behind]

STOKE POGES - ST. GILES' CHURCH
STOKE PARK

In the Domesday Book, Stoke Poges is listed as Stoche, meaning 'hamlet'. The second part of the name refers to the Pogeys family, who held the manor in the 13th century. Queen Elizabeth I was entertained at the original manor house in 1601, though King Charles I was not so fortunate, as this was one of the places in which he was held prisoner in the years before his execution. In the following century the manor was held by Thomas Penn, son of the founder of Pennsylvania, and remained in the Penn family for more than a century.

[The final resting place of Teresa Bond in *For Your Eyes Only*]

Parts of St. Giles' Church, which stands in the grounds of the manor, date back to Saxon times, and much of the tower and chancel are Norman. It is believed that Thomas Gray's *Elegy Written in a Country Churchyard* was penned here in 1750 (although this is disputed by some who cite Everdon in Northamptonshire as being the correct churchyard). However, what is not in dispute is that Gray is buried at St. Giles', and there is a large monument in the adjoining field (called Gray's Field and belonging to the National Trust) displaying the Elegy. It is to the church and field that the reader should go, since this was the location used in the opening shots of *For Your Eyes Only*. It is here that Bond is seen emerging from the lychgate, and turning left, lays some roses on the grave of his wife. The grave is inscribed with the words, 'Teresa Bond, 1943-1969, Beloved wife of James Bond, We have all the time in the World',a rather touching reminder of *On Her Majesty's Secret Service* in which, it will be remembered, Irma Bunt kills Teresa in a drive-by shooting as she sets off on honeymoon with Bond. It will also be recalled that Louis Armstrong sings *We Have All the Time in the World* in that film, and that in both the film and book these are the last words spoken by Bond.

Bond is soon interrupted by the vicar who informs him that his office has called, that there is some kind of emergency, and that they are sending a helicopter to pick him up. Next the viewer sees a Universal Exports helicopter landing at Gray's Field into which Bond gets and flies off with the vicar making the sign of the cross, rather ominously, as the helicopter takes off.

A unique feature of the church is the Memorial Gardens, which have been designed so that they do not remind one of a cemetery. It was Sir Noel Mobbs, the Lord of the Manor, who purchased twenty acres of land to the south of the church to be a 'living memorial to the dead and of solace to the bereaved'. The gardens were designed by Edward White and have no buildings or monuments, but instead consist of small gardens and family plots (around five hundred gated plots in all). They were completed in 1937, and, following a major refurbishment starting in 2001, are now a Grade I listed Garden of Remembrance where one can stroll and appreciate the beauty and sheer magnificence of nature. If this is not of interest in itself the reader should walk to the east side of the gardens, which afford views across the lake of one of the most famous Bond locations of all – Stoke Park.

["Strict rules of golf, Goldfinger?" Between the Repton Bridge and the back of the clubhouse is the 18th green where the game between Bond and Goldfinger reaches its climax.]

The ownership of the Stoke Park Estate can be traced back to before the Domesday Book. In 1581 it became the property of the Crown in payment for debts of Henry Hastings, the 3rd Earl of Huntingdon, whose father had been the Commander in Chief of King Henry VIII's army. However, it was John Penn who was responsible for most of what can be seen today, paying for it largely from the £13,000 that the United States Government paid him for the twenty-six million acre plot in Pennsylvania. The mansion, which deliberately has more than a passing resemblance to the White House in Washington D.C., was designed by James Wyatt between 1790 and 1813, while the landscape, some three hundred and fifty acres, was designed by Capability Brown and Humphry Repton in 1792.

The estate was used as a private residence until 1908 when Nick 'Pa' Lane Jackson, founder of the Corinthian Sporting Club, purchased the estate and turned it into Britain's first country club. The golf course was designed by Harry Colt and opened in 1909 to great acclaim. Today it is ranked in the top one hundred courses in the world, with the exceptional quality of the greens being a major feature.

On the small screen Stoke Park can be seen in *The Vice*, *The Professionals*, *Pie in the Sky*, *Midsomer Murders*, *Foyle's War* and *Dead of Night*. The mini break with Hugh Grant and rowing scenes from *Bridget Jones's Diary* (2001) were all filmed here, as were scenes from *Wimbledon* (2004), *Bride and Prejudice* (2004), *RocknRolla* (2008) and *Layer Cake* (2004). The latter film is of particular significance since the dramatic ending on the mansion steps featured one Daniel Craig.

The ballroom made an appearance in *Tomorrow Never Dies* as Bond's hotel room in Hamburg, where Paris Carver is later found dead on the bed and where Bond subsequently meets Doctor Kaufman, whose hobby it transpires is torture.

Of course the most famous appearance of Stoke Park is without doubt in *Goldfinger*. Bond meets Goldfinger at his country club (literally as it later transpires) and joins him in a game. The golf shop where the two first meet is no longer in existence, but the rest of the sequence can still be seen today.

The two play to the 16th hole at which point Goldfinger suggests to Bond that he is not there merely to play golf. Bond drops a Nazi gold bar onto the green, which puts Goldfinger off his putt. It is now, with the game all square, that Goldfinger takes the bait and challenges Bond to play the last two holes for the gold bar, or at least the cash equivalent, which is considerably more than the original bet of a shilling a hole suggested by

Bond in the golf shop! However, Bond accepts the wager. Goldfinger's next shot goes into the rough, and while searching for the lost golf ball Bond finds another, a Slazenger 7. It is now that Bond discovers that, as with cards, Goldfinger cheats, as Oddjob miraculously find's Goldfinger's Slazenger 1 ball next to the fairway. Bond, though, is not above cheating himself, for when his caddy clearly doubts that the ball found is Goldfinger's, Bond replies confidently that it is not, since he is standing on it. The hole is halved and Bond switches Goldfinger's Slazenger 1 for the Slazenger 7 that he found. The final hole is played with Goldfinger winning, or at least until Bond notices that Goldfinger has been using the wrong ball and that since "we are playing strict rules … I'm afraid you lose the hole and the match'.

The final sequence takes place in front of the clubhouse, as Bond is admiring Goldfinger's Phantom Three 37 Rolls Royce, onto which he surreptitiously attaches a homing device. Goldfinger banters with Bond, saying that he a clever and resourceful man, and that he hopes that their paths will not cross again. By way of demonstration that he is not a man to be meddled with, Goldfinger has Oddjob decapitate one of the statues with his bowler hat.

[Statue outside the clubhouse (left)]

Similar statues still adorn the front of the clubhouse, but this special effect was actually created at Pinewood Studios (page 45). Bond coolly quips, "Remarkable, but what does the club secretary have to say?" – to which Goldfinger equally coolly replies, "Nothing, Mr. Bond. I own the club."
The scene finishes with Goldfinger paying his gambling debt to Bond by writing out a cheque to cash for £5,000, and Bond returning Goldfinger's Slazenger 1 to Oddjob, who duly crushes it in his hand. So ends one of the most memorable ten minute sequences of any Bond film, which for its success relies entirely on character and good dialogue over special effects and expensive sets.

Finally it is interesting to note that it was here that Sean Connery was first introduced to golf, a game that he has been quoted as saying is more important to him than acting. Both Connery and Barbara Broccoli are members of the club.

[The front of Stoke Park where Goldfinger's Rolls Royce was parked, taken from where the golf shop used to stand]

STOWE - STOWE LANDSCAPE GARDENS

The parish of Stowe, near Buckingham, originally comprised four villages, but only one, Dadford, survives. The others, including the village of Stowe, have vanished. Today Stowe is famous for the public school, which occupies Stowe House, and for the landscaped gardens, with their various temples and follies, owned by the National Trust since 1989. Stowe may have been a sacred place in Anglo-Saxon times. At all events, after the Norman conquest, the manor was given to Odo, the Bishop of Bayeux – who happened to be William the Conqueror's half-brother – and not long after 1086 the manor became the property of a college of secular canons in Oxford, the transfer being confirmed in 1130 by a charter of King Henry I.

By 1150 the Augustine Osney Abbey had absorbed the college, and its ownership of Stowe lasted until the Dissolution of the Monasteries in 1539. Three years later it became the property of the diocese of Oxford when Osney Abbey was consecrated a cathedral. In 1590 it was given to Queen

Elizabeth I, who in turn granted it new secular owners, who subsequently sold it to John Temple. In 1651 his grandson enclosed the area and made it into a deer park. It was at about this time that the village was abandoned. The estate remained in the Temple-Grenville family until 1921 when the Reverend Luis C. F. T. Morgan Grenville, due to prodigious debts, was forced to sell the house, gardens and part of the park to Harry Shaw for the sum of £50,000.

[The Gothic Temple, minus Scottish piper, from the funeral scene of Sir Robert King in *The World Is Not Enough*]

Shaw was unable to find enough money to maintain the building, which was consequently sold the following year to the governors of what is today Stowe School. The rest of the estate was sold in small lots, one, the Grand Avenue, being purchased by the famous architect, Clough Williams-Ellis, in order to prevent it being turned into housing. He later donated it to the school, which was also responsible for the gardens. Finally in 1989 an anonymous donor provided funds for an endowment, and the National Trust assumed ownership of what is now known as Stowe Landscape Gardens.

A modest formal parterre garden which existed at Stowe in the 1690s has not survived. Within a few years it had given way to by Lord Cobham's widely acclaimed baroque park, created initially by Charles Bridgeman and John Vanbrugh, to which William Kent later added temples, bridges and other structures, his masterwork being the Elysian Fields, with its Temples of Ancient Virtue and of British Worthies. In 1741 Capability Brown became head gardener, creating the Grecian Valley and the Hawkwell Field, which features James Gibbs' Gothic Temple.

The Gothic Temple, designed in 1741 and completed around 1748, is the only building in the gardens built from ironstone. The building is triangular with a pentagonal tower at each corner. Above the main door is a quote from Pierre Corneille's play *Horace*, which translated reads, 'I thank the gods I am not a Roman'. The interior includes a circular room of two stories covered by a shallow dome, painted so as to look like a mosaic, including shields representing the Heptarchy. In the 1930s the temple was used by the school as the armoury for the Officer Training Corps, but today you can rent it out as a holiday home via The Landmark Trust.

In *The World Is Not Enough* a Scottish piper plays a lament from the top of the tower, during which the funeral procession of Sir Robert King is passing out of the temple and along a line of trees below. This is the first time we see Bond, M and Elektra King together at what is supposed to be the King estate. This is obviously meant to be in Scotland since the next shot is of Eilean Donan Castle (page 215) with the subtitle indicating that this is MI6's Scottish base.

Other productions that have used the area include *Indiana Jones and the Last Crusade* (1989) in which the North Front doubles as Berlin, and where Jones encounters Hitler, *Vanity Fair*, which used the gardens to represent Hyde Park, *Stardust* (2007) and *The Wolfman* (2010).

Stowe is one of the most remarkable creations of Georgian England and has inspired writers, philosophers, artists, politicians and members of the public for hundreds of years. Today there are over forty temples and monuments to explore from a variety of walks that are open year round.

For further information see www.nationaltrust.org.uk/stowe.

WADDESDON - WADDESDON MANOR

[Waddesdon Manor in bloom]

To call Waddesdon Manor a country house is somewhat of an understatement – it is actually a neo-renaissance building in the style of a French chateau, as found in the Loire Valley, with a large estate around it. Ornate luxury comes to mind when looking at the magnificent large mansion, not a surprise considering that it was built for Baron Ferdinand de Rothschild. His chosen architect was Gabriel-Hippolyte Destailleur.

It may look old-fashioned on the outside, but on the inside, the Baron had the most modern innovations of the 19th century incorporated, such as a steel frame, which permits the layout of the upper floors to be totally different from that of the lower floors. It also has hot and cold running water in its bathrooms, central heating and an electric bell system as well as electric lighting. The Manor housed an extensive French 18th century collection of fine art as well as English and Dutch paintings, some of which were passed on to the British Museum as the 'Waddesdon Bequest' after the Baron died in 1898.

The gardens were landscaped extensively, under the guidance of the French landscape architect Lainé. Not a mean feat as the hilltop was barren, and several fully-grown trees were planted, some so big it took sixteen horses to move them to their new location. It is regarded as one of the finest Victorian gardens in Britain. Queen Victoria invited herself to view the park, but is reported to have been more fascinated by the new invention of electric lighting that had been installed – it is said that she spent ten minutes switching a chandelier on and off. While some collections were bequeathed, following generations of Rothschilds have added to the fine art and furniture collections, and they continue to be a draw for visitors.

The grounds and property have been owned by the National Trust (www.waddesdon.org.uk) since 1957, but continue to be administered by a Rothschild family trust as a semi-independent operation, which is an unprecedented arrangement – normally the National Trust does that itself once it takes ownership of a property and former owners tend to be no longer involved. James de Rothschild bequeathed the Manor and its contents along with two hundred acres of grounds and the largest ever endowment to the National Trust – £750,000. Eythrope and the rest of the Waddesdon estate remain in the Rothschild family's possession. The Rothschilds tended to reside around the borders of Hertfordshire and Buckinghamshire, an area unofficially known as 'Rothschildshire', and at one point they owned seven large country houses and thirty thousand acres of land in the area, and further afield another forty great Rothschild properties across Europe. The current baron, Jacob Rothschild, 4th Lord Rothschild, has overseen a major restoration and introduced new collections.

On 10th June 2003, approximately one hundred, irreplaceable and priceless, French gold snuff boxes and bejewelled trifles were stolen, none of which has thus far been recovered. There is still a reward on offer for information leading to their recovery.

Films that made use of the stunning house and gardens include, *Carry On Don't Lose Your Head* (1966), *An Ideal Husband* (1999), *Daniel Deronda* (2002), *The Tenth Kingdom* (2000) and *The Queen* (2006) starring Dame Helen Mirren, where it stood in for Buckingham Palace gardens. James Bond visited Waddesdon in *Never Say Never Again*. The interior became the casino in Nice where Largo is hosting a charity event, and where he and Bond play the Domination video game (eventually won by Bond but not without considerable pain), and where later Bond dances with Domino, informing her that her brother is dead. It is also where earlier in the film the SPECTRE members, including Fatima Blush, meet to hear their esteemed No. 1 outline the plan known as the Tears of Allah.

JAMES BOND IN CAMBRIDGESHIRE
WANSFORD - NENE VALLEY RAILWAY

[A wagon-lits, similar to that used by Octopussy, waiting to depart Wansford station on the Nene Valley Railway close to where Bond helps load Octopussy's train]

The village of Wansford lies just off the Great North Road (A1) between Peterborough and Stamford in the very north-east corner of the county. Wansford is in fact two separate villages under different parish councils, Huntingdon and Peterborough. The boundary is half way across the twelve arch bridge spanning the River Nene. The seven northern arches date from 1577, the next three from 1672-4 while the final two were not added until 1795. Daniel Defoe wrote glowingly of the bridge itself but was not so appreciative of the toll imposed by Lord Fitzwilliam of two shillings and six pence saying that ''tis the only half crown toll that is in Britain'.

The village is picturesque, most of the buildings being built of limestone with roofs of Collyweston stone or thatch. The main public house is the Haycock Hotel, a former coaching inn dating from 1571, originally called the Swan Inn. It has some fifty bedrooms which seems out of all proportion for such a small village.

The river was once the route that carried local produce to Peterborough, and its south bank was lined with warehouses and granaries, which, after the arrival of the railway, were converted to housing. Wansford had its own paper mill, making paper from recycled rags for among others *The Times*, in a building known as the Soll, but it closed in 1855 after an explosion.

Today, Wansford's main attraction is the Nene Valley Railway, whose headquarters is at Wansford station. The NVR is a preserved standard gauge railway, running seven and a half miles between Yarwell Junction and Peterborough, where the line's own station, Peterborough Nene Valley, was opened in 1986, next to the Railworld Museum. The line, constructed by the London & Birmingham Railway, originally ran from Blisworth in Northamptonshire to Peterborough. It was completed in 1847, but it remained an insignificant route until another line was built some decades later, through Nassington and King's Cliffe to Seaton, below Welland Viaduct, and Wansford became an important junction. Later still, a third line was constructed, via Sutton and Barnack to Stamford, on the Midland Railway. From 1900 to 1960 the Nene Valley line carried a good deal of traffic between East Anglia and the Midlands, and passengers from Wansford were ideally placed to travel by train to almost any part of the country.

However, the line was never classed as a major route, and in the 1960s it fell victim to Dr. Beeching's axe. By 1966 all passenger services had been withdrawn, though freight traffic continued until 1972. The preservation of the NVR had already been set in motion, however, thanks to the Reverend Richard Paten, who in 1968 had purchased a British Railways Standard Class '5' 4-6-0 locomotive, which he had restored to full working order. In 1969 the East Anglian Locomotive Society, shortly to become the Peterborough Locomotive Society, was formed, and in 1971 the Reverend Paten's engine was moved to the British Sugar Corporation's sidings at Fletton, where it was joined by *Jack's Green*, a Hunslet 0-6-0 locomotive. That same year the Locomotive Society changed its name to the Peterborough Railway Society, and adopted the plan of running trains once more along the Nene Valley line.

In 1974 the Peterborough Development Corporation purchased the line between Longville and Yarwell Junction and leased it to the Peterborough Railway Society – in essence the NVR had been born, although it was not to be officially called that until 1977. One problem faced by the society was that all the good British locomotive stock had already been purchased by other preservation groups. The solution was to seek out Continental engines and rolling stock instead. The only potential difficulty was that the loading gauge is larger for such stock, necessitating the demolition of one bridge and alterations to the width to some station platforms. As a consequence the Wansford Steam Centre opened in 1974. The track was upgraded for passenger traffic, and the first passenger train ran on the 1st June 1977 hauled by Nord, a French locomotive and '1178' a Swedish tank locomotive. By 1986 the line had been extended into Peterborough to its current terminus. Today the NVR has in the region of thirty locomotives and operates most weekends from March to November, as well as other days during the summer months, and for Santa Specials on selected dates towards Christmas. For full details please visit the NVR website, www.nvr.org.uk.

Largely because of its Continental rolling stock, the NVR featured in many television and film productions, including several episodes of *Secret Army* between 1977 and 1979. In 1989 the rock band Queen shot a video entitled *Breakthru* at the railway. It reached a respectable number seven in the British pop charts. Hercule Poirot, in the form of David Suchet, spent three days here filming the remake of *Murder on the Orient Express* using some Belgian coaching stock along with the Reverend Paten's locomotive, now named *City of Peterborough*. Episodes of *Eastenders* and *Casualty* have also been filmed here.

[The spot where Bond helps to load Octopussy's train]

By far the largest film production to visit the NVR was for *Octopussy*, when the line became the border area between East and West Germany, through which Octopussy's Flying Circus train passes. The first shot shows Bond helping to load Octopussy's train at Wansford station, with the signal box clearly visible in the background.

[Red Octopussy CCTs are still very much in evidence at the NVR (top). Looking under the A1 towards where General Orlov boards the train to inspect the jewels prior to switching them (bottom)]

Next General Orlov is seen emerging from the sidings and onto the platform. He enters a small four-wheel red utility truck, with a red brick bridge, actually the main A1 dual carriageway, in the background. The wagon in question is a London Midland and Scottish Railway Covered Carriage Truck (CCT), van number 37066, which was specially adapted for the film, having ribs to the roof, personnel doors at each end, grab rails on the side and a hatch in the roof added.

[The Wansford end of the Wansford tunnel where the jewels are switched for an atomic bomb]

Bond continues his observation of the goings on from his position under the CCT, which is soon to be moved by a shunting locomotive, named *Horsa*, into the six hundred and sixteen yards long Wansford tunnel, where there is another identical CCT waiting. The difference is that this one contains a hundred ton nuclear yield atomic bomb in place of the casket of jewels. As the substitute wagon is shunted off to join Octopussy's train, Bond climbs aboard the CCT containing the jewels, which he finds are being removed by one of the twin knife-throwers, whom Bond is able to dispatch without too much trouble, placing his body down the barrel of the circus cannon.

The action now switches to the Yarwell end of the tunnel, where Orlov is waiting for the wagon with the jewels to emerge from the tunnel. He descends some steps at the side of the tunnel entrance, which were built especially for the filming and no longer exist, in order to retrieve the canister with the booty. This is done for him by two soldiers who are instructed to place it in his Mercedes car, parked above the tunnel portal. Orlov then climbs aboard the CCT only to find Bond, dressed as the knife-throwing twin, waiting for him. Luckily for Orlov a soldier returns to the wagon, allowing the General to escape back into the tunnel where he boards *Horsa*, leaving a gunfight to ensue between the soldiers and Bond.

James Bond in Cambridgeshire

At this point a train whistle is heard, indicating that Octopussy's train is departing. The only course of action left to Bond, once the soldiers have been dealt with, or evaded, is to climb the steps and requisition Orlov's now unguarded car.

[The Yarwell end of the tunnel where the gunfight ensues (top) and the sidings through which Bond drives Orlov's Mercedes (bottom)]

80

[Two views of the level crossing at Wansford where Bond skids the Mercedes onto the railway line in pursuit of Octopussy's train]

Bond then drives rather recklessly back down to Wansford station, going through the sidings and what is now the main car park. At one point Bond has the car on just two wheels, as he famously did previously in *Diamonds Are Forever*, in order to avoid the bullets from the East German soldiers firing at him. He continues to the main road, but not before he has gone over a car trap, which completely removes all four tyres. It is now time for another improbable stunt, as the car skids at the level crossing onto the railway track. It transpires that Mercedes build their cars with a wheelbase of exactly the same width as British standard gauge railway track – four feet eight-and-a-half inches. General Orlov now appears in another Mercedes, giving his somewhat surprised driver the instruction to "follow that car" as Bond disappears on the railway track over the Wansford bridge towards Peterborough.

[Orton Mere station from both ends, clearly showing the signal box where the signalman switches Bond onto the other track allowing him to come alongside Octopussy's train]

82

James Bond in Cambridgeshire

[The camera angle used to shoot the catapulting Mercedes over the train and into the River Nene]

Next, Bond is Bond is seen cruising along the single track in the vicinity of Orton Mere, at the Peterborough end of the line. As he passes the station signal box, the signalman switches the points to divert him on to the other track, and he passes through the station, much to the astonishment of the travellers waiting on the platform. Soon he draws alongside Octopussy's train and, fixing an umbrella to hold the accelerator pedal in place, is able to climb through the sunroof and jump onto the CCT with the nuclear device inside. This, of course, is done just in time as a train approaching in the other direction smashes into Bond's car, sending it flying into a river, where there are further looks of astonishment from those fishing there, especially the man fishing in the boat which the Mercedes hits and sinks. This scene was shot back at Wansford, the car actually being catapulted over a train as it passed over the bridge. The careful observer will spot the Wansford signal box in the background.

Soon General Gogol is on the scene as the car is very soon lifted out of the River Nene with the help of a crane. He discovers the jewels in the boot and knows instantly what has happened, departing by helicopter to stop Orlov before he can cross the border into West Germany. Meanwhile Orlov pursues Bond, who by now is safely aboard the train in the CCT, hiding in a gorilla costume as the border guards inspect the wagon, with Gobinda and the other knife throwing-twin in attendance. The scene comes to a climax at the border, with Orlov and Gogol's helicopter arriving simultaneously. Orlov runs after the train but is shot by one of the East German border guards. As the sequence ends, the furious Gogol denounces Orlov as "a common thief! A disgrace to his uniform!" Orlov has just enough breath to retort, "Yes. But tomorrow I shall be a hero of the Soviet Union!"

[Ferry Meadows the sight of the border crossing between East and West Germany]

This section was filmed at Ferry Meadows station, back along the line towards Wansford, the border crossing buildings being just props constructed for the filming and removed soon afterwards.

The rest of the antics aboard the train, or more correctly outside and on top of the train, as Bond fights both Gobinda and the remaining knife-throwing twin, take place on the straight section of single track between Wansford and Ferry Meadows, with the Wansford tunnel again making an appearance.

Railway experts will note that the locomotive pulling Octopussy's train bears the number 62015, which belonged to a Gresley K1 class engine, built in 1949 and used for general duties. Unfortunately that locomotive was scrapped 1965. The locomotive we see on screen is actually a DSB S 740, late of the Danish State Railway. Twenty of these locomotives were build between 1924-8, chiefly for the local traffic around Copenhagen, Hillerod and Helsingor. Each weighed ninety-eight tons and had a maximum speed of fifty-five miles per hour. DSB S 740 was bought by Mike Bradley in 1979, and was resident at the NVR at the time of filming. In 1995 it returned to Denmark and is now owned by the Nordsjællands Veterantog, a Danish railway society. In the film the train was modified so as to appear to be a German type DRG-Baureihe 62. However, there is a problem here as well, since the last of this type of locomotive was retired in 1968 some fifteen years before the film.

[This straight section of track, as viewed from the Mill Lane bridge looking towards Wansford, was where much of the fight sequence on top of the carriages was filmed]

A dozen years later the Bond production team returned to the NVR to film a key sequence for *GoldenEye*. This time the setting doubled for St. Petersburg, where Alec Trevelyan kept his luxury armoured train stored in the sidings. In fact the locomotive was a modified British Railway's Class 20 diesel, number D8188. This engine, built in 1967 and weighing seventy-two tons, is still operational and is currently a resident at the Severn Valley Railway.

[British Sugar still have offices in Peterborough]

Bond is in his tank (page 139) when he first sees the train, with Xenia Onatopp emerging from the driving cab, as General Ourumov and Natalya Simonova arrive by car and she is bundled on board. It is surrounded by what looks like a factory complex and is in fact the old British Sugar sidings at Fletton, where the Reverend Paten first stabled his locomotive. Although British Sugar is still based in the area nothing remains of the industrial complex, which was all redeveloped into housing just after filming in 1995.

In the next scene Ourumov, Simonova and Trevelyan are all seen in a luxury carriage reminiscent of the wagon-lits used by Octopussy, as the train passes a rather drab looking Ferry Meadows station (with no sign of the border crossing from *Octopussy*). Meanwhile Bond seems to have somehow got in front of the train and is emerging from a railway tunnel in his tank, blocking the line ahead of Trevelyan. The latter decides to ram the tank and orders the driver to use full speed. Bond fires a shot at the train before departing the tank to take cover along the trackside. The train, with the locomotive on fire, crashes into the tank, destroying it but coming to a halt, allowing Bond to board, rescue Simonova and kill Ourumov, while

Trevelyan and Onatopp escape by the helicopter concealed in one of the carriages. However, there is just time for Trevelyan to set a self destruct timer with the bomb exploding just after Bond and Simonova exit the train. The latter asks Bond, "Do you destroy every vehicle you get into?".

[Location of the tunnel portal, built abutting the bridge, in *GoldenEye*]

In this case the tunnel used was not that at Wansford but merely a fibreglass extension added to the Peterborough side of the bridge at Mill Lane.

JAMES BOND IN CORNWALL
BODELVA - EDEN PROJECT

[Perhaps the most unusual looking diamond mine in the world (with the new educational centre in the foreground)?]

The Eden Project is far more than just a futuristic looking visitor attraction situated in an old clay pit around three miles from St. Austell, a town known for as the centre of the English china clay industry.

The site, boasting the world's largest greenhouse and rainforest in captivity with steamy jungles and waterfalls, consists of two artificial biomes containing plants collected from all around the world, so that each enclosure emulates a natural biome, from a tropical rainforest to a Mediterranean environment. Each dome consists of hundreds of hexagonal and pentagonal, inflated, plastic cells supported by steel frames. Glass was not used because of the weight involved, so instead plastic cladding created from layers of UV-transparent ETFE film was utilised. The sheets are sealed around the perimeter and then inflated to create a large cushion that also acts as a thermal insulator for the biomes.

The whole project was conceived by Tim Smit and designed by Nicholas Grimshaw. It took two-and-a-half years to construct and opened to the public in March 2001 (although a visitor centre did open in May 2000).

Once in the attraction there is a meandering path with views of the two biomes, planted landscapes and sculptures (including a giant bee and a towering robot made up from old electrical appliances).

The Tropical Rainforest Biome is one hundred and eighty feet tall and covers an area of almost four acres; the specimens it contains include banana trees, coffee, rubber and bamboo plants. The Mediterranean Biome, featuring plants such as olives and grape vines, is less than half the size. Tea, lavender, hops, hemp, sunflowers and other temperate plants can be found in the Outdoor Biome (not covered). The educational facility, called the Core, which opened in 2005, has a unique copper-clad roof whose design derives from phyllotaxis, the 'opposing spirals' that are the mathematical basis of nearly all plant life and are perhaps most noticeable in pine cones and pineapples.

[The biome roofs through which Jinx gains entry to the mine]

The Eden Project has featured in several documentaries, and some sections of the 2009 television serial *The Day of the Triffids* were shot there, but cinemagoers will recognise it from *Die Another Day*. Interior scenes of Gustav Graves's Icelandic diamond mine (conveniently next door to his Ice Palace, modelled on the famous Ice Palace Hotel at Jukkasjärvi in Sweden) were filmed in the Tropical Rainforest Biome in March 2002. The viewer should not be fooled for much of what is seen was filmed back at Pinewood Studios (page 45).

For further information, opening times and admission prices please visit the Eden Project website at www.edenproject.com.

NEWQUAY - HOLYWELL BAY

[Visitors today will see no sign of barricades or the North Korean army patrolling the beach]

Around three miles southwest of Newquay can be found Holywell Bay. This magnificent beach adjoins Penhale Camp, an army training establishment regularly used by cadets, while on the north side is Holywell Cave, which is accessible at low tide and contains many pools formed by the natural build up of minerals. Tourists are attracted by the mile-long expanse of golden sand and the rich blue of the sea. Over seventy years ago, in his book *Walking in Cornwall*, J. R. A. Hockin noted that this beach is reckoned to be the sweetest bay in England.

It was for this very reason that the *Die Another Day* production crew had James Bond, and his two colleagues, arriving here by surf board in the film's pre-title sequence. For this scene, supposedly somewhere along the Pukch'ong coast in North Korea, some of the filming was done here, although the major surfing shots were filmed at Peahi in Hawaii. When we first see Bond he is taking a short rest to get his breath back – and no wonder! Then he sets off again on his mission, much of which was filmed in Hampshire.

A famous local resident was W. J. Burley, the author of the *Wycliffe* novels who lived in Holywell right up until his death in 2002.

JAMES BOND IN EAST SUSSEX

EASTBOURNE - BEACHY HEAD

[The Beachy Head lighthouse close to where Bond jumps from the exploding Land Rover in *The Living Daylights*]

Beachy Head, near Eastbourne, juts into the sea on the eastern side of Birling Gap – the opposite side from the cliffs called the Seven Sisters. It is the highest chalk cliff sea in Britain, and from its summit, five hundred and thirty feet above sea level, one can see as far as Dungeness to the east and Selsey Bill to the east. On a clear day even the Isle of Wight is visible. Its height has unfortunately also made it one of the most notorious suicide spots in the world. Indeed, the Maritime and Coastguard Agency have patrols around the clock looking for people acting suspiciously, and in turn pass on any information to the Chaplaincy Team, who then investigate further. The headland was named as 'Beauchef', meaning 'beautiful head (or chief)' in 1274. By 1724 the name had become the one we know today, Beachy Head, though it has nothing to do with beaches.

The chalk in this area was formed in the Late Cretaceous period, between sixty-five and a hundred million years ago, when the area was under the sea. During the Cenozoic Era the chalk was uplifted, and when the last Ice Age ended, the sea levels rose and the English Channel formed, cutting into the chalk to form the dramatic cliffs seen today. However, wave action contributes towards the erosion of cliffs around Beachy Head, which experience frequent small rock falls.

In 1929 an area of four thousand acres was bought by the borough of Eastbourne at a cost of £100,000, in order to save it from development. It now forms part of the Seven Sisters Country Park. One of the most interesting buildings along this coast is the Belle Tout lighthouse, which began operating in 1834. Sadly it proved less efficient than was hoped, as the light was often obscured by sea mists, so the present Beachy Head lighthouse was built at sea level, becoming operational in 1902. It was automated in 1983. Coastal erosion endangered the Belle Tout light, and in 1999 the entire structure was moved nearly thirty yards inland, provision being made for further moves if necessary. The Belle Tout is now a hotel.

Turning attention to filming, nearby Eastbourne, with its period residences and famous literary residents, such as Charles Dickens, Lewis Carroll and George Orwell, has appeared in many television productions, such as *Poirot*, *Foyle's War* and *Marple*, while on the big screen it recently doubled for its larger neighbour in *Brighton Rock* (2010). However, Beachy Head itself has appeared in the 2009 television adaptation of *Emma*, in two episodes of the cult series *The Prisoner* (with the Beachy Head lighthouse actually becoming a rocket and taking off in one of those episodes!), the rock opera *Quadrophenia* (1979), *Save Tomorrow* (2007), *Smokescreen* (1964), *Thicker than Water* (2005) and most memorably in the television serial *The Life and Loves of a She-Devil* in which the main character, Mary Fisher, played by Patricia Hodge lives in the Belle Tout lighthouse. It was also here that the Quidditch World Cup took place in *Harry Potter and the Goblet of Fire* (2005).

Whereas most of the pre-title sequence in *The Living Daylights* takes place on location in Gibraltar, from the moment the Land Rover smashes through the wall until it explodes just after Bond parachutes out of it, the location is either a studio set (for close ups) or Beachy Head. Vehicles were catapulted over the cliff, with dummies being extracted by fishing line to release the parachute upon exiting. The first shot was scrapped due to onlookers being visible in the background, and the filming ran into difficulties when the boat at the bottom of the cliffs positioned to film the descent got into difficulty in the heavy swell. In the event the Eastbourne lifeboats were launched to pull the crew off the cliffs, resulting in bravery awards for some members.

Even after filming had finished, the production crew had work to do, as the contract stipulated that the scattered remains of all the vehicles that had been flung over the cliff must be collected and removed from the shore, nearly five hundred and fifty feet below.

Desmond Llewellyn, who lived nearby at Bexhill, attended the first screening at the Curzon Cinema in Eastbourne, bringing some Bond gadgets for display. Before the film began, he presented the lifeboat crew with their bravery awards.

JAMES BOND IN ESSEX
STANSTED MOUNTFITCHET - STANSTED AIRPORT

[The Inflite hangar at Stansted Airport, doubling as Hamburg Airport, where James Bond picks up his BMW hire car and tries out the remote control system in *Tomorrow Never Dies*]

Although London Stansted Airport is the newest of the main London airports, its story actually began in 1942, when, as R.A.F. Stansted Mountfitchet, it was allocated to the U.S.A.A.F. Eighth Air Force as a bomber base and a major maintenance depot for B-26 bombers. After D-Day, these activities were moved to France, and the base served as a supply storage area, supporting aircraft on the continent. When the Americans left in August 1945, the Air Ministry transferred Stansted to No. 263 Maintenance Unit, R.A.F. for storage purposes. From March 1946 to August 1947, the airfield also housed German prisoners of war.

In 1949 the Ministry of Civil Aviation took over, and Stansted became the home of several charter airlines. Five years later, when plans were afoot to turn the airfield into a NATO base, the Americans returned and extended the runway. The proposed transfer to NATO did not happen, and Stansted continued as a centre of civil aviation, coming under the control of the British Airports Authority in 1966. From the 1960s to the early 1980s Stansted was home to the Civil Aviation Authority's Fire Service Training School, where all British and many foreign aviation fire crews were trained.

Meanwhile holiday charter traffic started to increase, and the first passenger terminal was opened in 1969. The largest change took place in 1984 when the government approved a two-phase development to make Stansted the third London airport, with an eventual capacity of fifteen million passengers per year. Construction took place between 1988 and 1991 with what for the time was a futuristic building of glass and steel designed by Lord Foster at a cost of £100 million.

Initially American Airlines provided flights between Stansted and Chicago, but these proved unprofitable and withdrawn in 1993. Later in the decade Continental Airlines operated services between Stansted and Newark, but they too were stopped shortly after the 9/11 attacks in 2001. In 2005, MAXjet Airways and Eos Airlines both launched all-business-class flights to New York, and two years later American Airlines returned to Stansted, but MAXjet ceased trading in December 2007 and Eos in April 2008, and in July 2008 American Airlines withdrew from Stansted. Finally, from June to August 2010, Sun Country Airlines instituted weekly flights to Minneapolis, with a refuelling stop in Gander, Newfoundland, but in 2011 Sun Country relocated to Gatwick.

Services to Europe have been more successful, but although in 2006-2007 the airport came close to handling its permitted maximum of twenty-five million passengers a year, numbers have fallen since then, and in 2012 there were less than eighteen million. The busiest airline operating from Stansted is the low-cost Ryanair. In 2008 plans were put forward for a second runway but these were abandoned in 2010, although this is still a long term objective of the airport owners.

Stansted is the airport designated by the government for handling aviation emergencies and crises, notably hijackings. In 2000 a hijacked Ariana Afghan Airlines Boeing 727 with one hundred and fifty-six people on board was diverted here, and after a four-day stand-off all passengers were all released safely.

Get Him to the Greek (2010), *Last Chance Harvey* (2008), *Flight 93* (2006), *London Dreams* (2009) and *Bugs* (2006) have all featured the main airport buildings. However, there are also various hangars and cargo buildings around the perimeter of the airfield. These include those belonging to Inflite and Titan Airways. The latter operates contract and *ad-hoc* passenger and freight charters throughout the world at short notice, which have included ferrying the Rolling Stones, Liverpool Football Club and the Prime Minister to various locations around the world. It also works on behalf of cruise ship companies such as Olsen Cruises, Princess Cruises and Cunard and has a regular contract with the Ministry of Defence to run a twice-weekly service to the Falkland Islands.

The Inflite Executive Jet Centre on the western perimeter is a family-run business offering the ultimate 'one stop shop' for the Corporate and Business Aircraft Operator. It provides an extensive range of aircraft handling, engineering and support services, all from its purpose built and newly refurbished premises.

["Grow up, 007," says Q to James Bond inside this very hangar after Bond shows off his skills with the car remote control. The Swissair plane under maintenance is hardly noticeable in the background.]

Most recently Inflite was responsible for ferrying the *Skyfall* production crew to location filming in Turkey. One of their hangars also has a place in James Bond film history, as this is where Bond takes delivery of his BMW 750 from Q in *Tomorrow Never Dies*, having already taken care of 'the insurance damage waiver for your beautiful new car' at the Avis rental desk on the main concourse at Hamburg Airport.

Q, you will recall, is particularly proud of the remote control feature, which he describes as surprisingly tricky to use. He may have found it so, but Bond soon gets to grips with it, and gives a demonstration of his driving skill that ends with the car screeching to a halt in front of them both (and just metres from a Titan Airways jet). As the scene ends, an exasperated Q tells Bond to 'grow up!'

SOUTHEND-ON-SEA - LONDON SOUTHEND AIRPORT

[The original 1960s control tower close to where James Bond in his Aston Martin DB5 watches Goldfinger leave for Geneva]

From the 1960s until the development of Stansted in the late 1970s, Southend-on-Sea was the country's third busiest airport in terms of passenger numbers (seven hundred thousand people in 1967). It is not surprising, then, that in the film *Goldfinger*, this was the airport from which the title character flew to Switzerland.

It was originally a Royal Flying Corps establishment during World War I, briefly belonging to the Royal Naval Air Service in 1915, until in 1916 if became R.F.C. Rochford. It was designated as a night fighter station, with many sorties being flown against Zeppelin airship raiders. After the war there was little use for an airfield in the area and so it was reverted to agricultural use in 1920. In 1935 it opened as Southend Municipal Airport. However, in 1939 it was reinstated as R.A.F. Rochford and became a base for fighter squadrons, comprising Spitfire, Hurricane and Blenheim aircraft. The airport had an underground control room, and to protect it from paratrooper attack some fifty pill boxes were built around the perimeter, many of which survive today.

The airfield was decommissioned in 1946 and once again became Southend Municipal Airport. It is best remembered for its car ferry flights, operated by the piston-engined Bristol Freighter and the Aviation Traders Carvair. It is also the place where Freddie Laker's Air Charter Limited started operations from in 1949. Passenger destinations in the 1950s included Newcastle, the Isle of Man, Ostend, Paris, Rochester, Rotterdam, Shoreham and the Channel Islands (operated by Channel Airways). By the 1960s Channel Airways had become one of the five leading independent British airlines, a position it held until the company ceased operating in 1972. One by one most of the scheduled airlines such as Dan-Air, British Air Ferries, British European Airways all moved away or were taken over by other larger companies, and in 1993, after making substantial losses, Southend Borough Council sold the airport to Regional Airports Limited, who renamed it London Southend Airport.

The airport became profitable under RAL, but proposals to extend the runway, allowing it to be used by larger and longer-range aircraft, were frustrated by the refusal of permission to move Eastwood parish church away from the main runway. The church, an important early mediaeval building, is now protected by a Grade 1 listing. In 2008 RAL sold the airport for £21 million to the Stobart Group, owner of Carlisle Airport, though best known as a road haulage company. As a condition of purchase and future investment by Stobart, permission was granted to increase the length of the runway by some three hundred metres and the upgrade the navigational aids and lighting infrastructure. In return the Stobart Group took out a loan of £100 million for the construction work, and by 2012 the airport had a new control tower, terminal building and railway station. In October that same year a four-star Holiday Inn, also owned by Stobart, opened next door to the airport entrance, and in November work began on an extension to the new terminal, to allow for the planned increase in passenger numbers. EasyJet now operates about seventy flights a week from Southend to various European destinations.

Southend Airport seems to have come full circle. In December 2012 EasyJet launched a seasonal service to Geneva – Auric Goldfinger's destination in the 1964 film. Today, though, the only kind of car allowed on board is a model one.

[Approximately the spot where Goldfinger boards the Carvair aeroplane bound for Geneva, watched by Bond in his Aston Martin to the very right of the picture]

In the film, it is a British United Air Ferries Carvair that transports Goldfinger and his car. However, as Bond later discovers that the car is made of gold – Goldfinger's audacious means of smuggling the precious metal out of Britain – we are entitled to wonder how the aeroplane got off the ground with all that extra weight.

[Vulcan XL426, without nuclear payload, awaiting restoration]

It has to be admitted that there are holes in the plot of this, one of the best and best-loved of the James Bond films. We may also wonder how Bond managed to place the magnetic tracking device on to Goldfinger's car, since gold is a non-ferrous metal and therefore non-magnetic. Bond is seen in his Aston Martin DB5, parked on the airport apron, with the wooden-clad control tower in the distance, watching Goldfinger's aeroplane take off. The in-car tracking device quite realistically shows a map of Southend-on-Sea, and a point of light correctly indicates the flight path. Less realistic is the airport official's statement, as he assures Bond that everything is all right because "I've got you booked out on the next flight to Geneva, leaving in half an hour." Even at the airport's busiest there were only around three flights a week to Geneva.

Since 1986 there has been a further James Bond connection with the airport, for the eastern side of the airfield is home to Avro Vulcan XL426, one of only three remaining such aircraft. It saw twenty-four years of service around the world and when just a year old set an unofficial record for flying the North Atlantic in only four hours and fifty-two minutes. It was bought in 1993 by the Vulcan Restoration Trust, who maintain the electronic systems and keep engines serviceable. Although it is not airworthy it is allowed to occasionally taxi and is open to the public periodically. It was of course a Vulcan loaded with two nuclear warheads that was hijacked by Largo in *Thunderball*.

JAMES BOND IN HAMPSHIRE

ALDERSHOT - BRUNEVAL BARRACKS EELMOOR DRIVER TRAINING AREA (LONG VALLEY)

[The currently disused Bruneval Barracks in Aldershot]

Aldershot is known today as the 'Home of the British Army', though its garrison dates only from 1854. There was a settlement here in Anglo-Saxon times, as its name (probably derived from 'Alder-holt', meaning a copse of alder trees) suggests. It is mentioned in the Domesday Book of 1086, but between then and 1850 Aldershot was little more than a large stretch of uncultivated common land, mostly useless for farming and with only a small scattered population. The stretch of the London to Winchester road that passed through the area was a notorious haunt of highway robbers, including, it is said, Dick Turpin.

When the army base was set up during the Crimean War, the population of Aldershot increased from less than one thousand in 1851 to sixteen thousand in 1861. Queen Victoria being a regular visitor, a Royal Pavilion was constructed for her, and for her Golden Jubilee Review in 1887, attended by royalty and other dignitaries from across the Empire and beyond, some sixty thousand troops lined up in the Long Valley, stretching from the Basingstoke Canal to Caesar's Camp. Between 1922 and 1939 the annual Aldershot Military Tattoo was famous for its sheer scale and spectacle.

The most notable Aldershot landmark is the Wellington Statue, which is thirty feet high and made of bronze from recycled cannons captured during the Battle of Waterloo. Originally the statue was on the Wellington Arch in London but Decimus Burton, the architect of the arch, thought it out of proportion, and Queen Victoria claimed that it ruined her view from Buckingham Palace and so without much debate it was moved to Aldershot.

Along the Farnborough Road are various barracks collectively and unimaginatively known as South Camp. Nine barracks were built originally but all save one of these Victorian brick buildings were demolished in the 1960s to make way for what became known as the Montgomery Lines. Four rather ugly barracks (Arnhem, Bruneval, Normandy Invasion and Rhine Crossing), all named after famous airborne actions in the Second World War, were built of concrete. Bruneval Barracks, named after an action that took place near Le Havre in February 1942, and now disused and boarded up pending redevelopment, became Kazan for the end sequence of *Quantum of Solace*, in which M learns that Bond can be trusted all along and that she needs him back in the service – to which the latter responds that he has never been away.

The barracks are also the site for the memorial to the seven people who were killed by the IRA on the 22nd February 1972, when the 16th Parachute Brigade Officers' Mess was bombed.

[James Bond, at least the stand-in for Pierce Brosnan, during the filming of *Die Another Day* at the Eelmoor Driver Training Area]

James Bond in Hampshire

To the north-west, close to Church Crookham, is Long Valley, which today is part of the Eelmoor Driver Training Area, a circular track approximately a mile in length used by the Ministry of Defence for training drivers of fast military vehicles. This proved to be the perfect site to double for North Korea in the earlier part of the hovercraft chase in *Die Another Day*, the latter part being filmed at Chinnor (page 143).

[It would appear that the best way to move a hovercraft into position is via a forklift truck]

[One of the Specially modified hovercraft used in filming]

CAMBERLEY - MINLEY TRAINING AREA

[Looking across the border between North and South Korea at the Hawley Bear Pit near Hawley Lake]

Camberley, actually just across the border in Surrey, is the closest town to the Minley Training Area in Hampshire, which includes what locals call the Hawley Bear Pit, close to Hawley Lake. Very much like Aldershot, the area was known to be the haunt of highwaymen, and was, due to the sandy topsoil, not considered worth farming. Indeed Daniel Defoe described the area as barren, sterile and 'horrid and frightful to look on, not only good for little, but good for nothing'. The town as it now stands has its roots in the building of The Royal Military College, now the Royal Military Academy Sandhurst, in 1812. A settlement grew up here that was originally called New Town, but in 1831 was renamed Yorktown, after Prince Frederick, Duke of York and Albany. Later the Cambridge Hotel was built by a property speculator and so the surrounding area became Cambridge Town, but was renamed Camberley in 1877 so as to avoid confusion with the rather more famous university town of the same name.

The Minley Training Area itself is in the main lowland heath, comprising conifer woods, areas of mature and semi-mature broadleaved woodland, mire, scrub, acid grassland and grass meadows, with parts being designated a Site of Special Scientific Interest and forming part of the European designated Thames Basin Heaths Special Protection Area. Public access is permitted along all public rights of way at all times, since any army exercises here do not involve live ammunition. The best place for the visitor to park is by the Hawley Lake Sail Training Centre, which is fifteen minutes' walk to the Hawley Bear Pit. This was the location used for the exchange of prisoners, shown just after the titles in *Die Another Day*. Bond, after fourteen months in a North Korean prison, is traded for Zoa, and walks to freedom across a bridge, supposedly between North and South Korea. For this shot a bridge across the 'Bear Pit' (which had to be filled with water), along with other buildings, was erected, and a fog generator employed to give the correct atmosphere, since the actual area is much smaller than one might imagine from looking at the film.

FARNBOROUGH - FARNBOROUGH AIRPORT

[Monument to Sir Frank Whittle with the airport building behind]

Farnborough, whose name derives from the Old English Ferneberga, meaning 'fern hill', forms a single conurbation with the neighbouring town of Aldershot. In 1881 Empress Eugénie founded St. Michael's Abbey here as a monument to her late husband, Napoleon III of France. Both of them, along with their son, now rest in the Imperial Crypt in granite sarcophagi provided by Queen Victoria.

Inextricably linked with Farnborough since the very earliest days of flight is the airfield. Samuel Franklin Cody was one of the original pioneers of aviation, making the first aeroplane flight in Britain in October 1908. He was to die on a subsequent flight, when he crashed his plane on Ball Hill, which is within the technology park that surrounds the airfield.

Another famous name associated with Farnborough is Sir Frank Whittle, who conducted much of his research into jet aircraft propulsion at the Royal Aircraft Establishment here. In fact there is even a replica of his prototype Gloster E28/39 sited on the roundabout just outside the gates to the airport along Ively Road, and just inside the main gate there is the stump of a large tree to which it is said Sir Frank used to tie his planes while testing the force produced by his engines. Such was experimental technique in those days.

Before the Royal Aircraft Establishment was opened in the early 20th century, Farnborough was home to His Majesty's Balloon Factory, also called the Army Balloon Factory, which in 1912 became the Royal Aircraft Factory. Among those who worked there were Geoffrey de Havilland, who went on to found his own company, and John Kenworthy, who became chief engineer at Austin Motors. The name was changed in 1918 to the Royal Aircraft Establishment, and so it remained until 1988, when in became the Royal Aerospace Establishment. Three years later it was merged with other research units to form the Defence Research Agency, which in turn became the Defence Evaluation and Research Agency in 1995 before being split into two organisations in 2001 – the state-owned Defence Science and Technology Laboratory and the commercial company QinetiQ. The aircraft developed or tested here included the Hurricane, the Harrier jump jet, and Concorde, as well as certain rocket projects and space satellites.

In 1991 the airfield itself was declared surplus to requirements by the Ministry of Defence, who decided that it should be redeveloped as a business aviation centre. Following a competitive process led by the government, TAG Aviation took control in 1997 and after much redevelopment and construction TAG Farnborough Airport Limited started operations in 2003, buying the freehold to the site in 2007. Perhaps the event most people know Farnborough for is the International Airshow, which has taken place here since 1948 and continues to be held every two years. The most recent airshow in 2012 drew over one hundred thousand trade visitors, with eighty military delegations from forty-six countries represented. Over one hundred and fifty aircraft took part and aviation business orders of around £45 billion were confirmed.

[The futuristic looking buildings at Farnborough Airport easily double for those of Brienz in Switzerland]

In *Quantum of Solace* Farnborough doubles for the airport at Bregenz in Austria, where Dominic Greene and James Bond arrive separately by private jet to attend a performance of Puccini's *Tosca* at Lake Constance. On the plane, you will remember, Greene meets Gregg Beam, the CIA's section chief for South America, and Felix Leiter. When Leiter is asked if he recognises Bond from a picture, he replies that he does not. Greene also confirms the deal he has made with Beam to control whatever resources his organisation finds in or under a seemingly worthless piece of desert in Bolivia, which Greene assumes is an oilfield. After a gunfight at the opera, Bond returns to the airport to follow Greene, but finds that M has had his passports and credit cards revoked, forcing him to make other arrangements. In turn, Bond misleads M as to his true intentions. He informs the woman at the check-in desk that she is about to receive a call, and asks her to say that he is *en route* to Cairo. She does so, willingly.

ODIHAM - R.A.F. ODIHAM

The historic village of Odiham, in the north-east part of the county, is recorded under the current spelling in the Domesday Book. In 1204 King John decided to build a castle here at a cost of over £1,000. It is thought that he considered the location strategic, as Odiham lies halfway between Windsor and Winchester. In 1216 the French Dauphin Louis VIII besieged King John in the castle for two weeks. By 1605 the castle was described as a ruin, and remains so to this day. Another old building in the village is the Pest House, which dates from 1622 and was used to house local people and travellers suffering from the plague. At this time there were many such 'isolation hospitals' in the country, but the Odiham Pest House is one of only five examples still remaining and today is a heritage centre. It was also in Odiham that on the 16th May 1783 a group of gentlemen along with what were described as some 'intelligent farmers' met at the George Inn to form a society dedicated to encouraging agriculture and industry in their village, and to reform animal care by establishing a school to teach veterinary science. The result was the foundation of the Royal Veterinary Society and the birth of the veterinary profession in Britain.

[A Chinook Mk3 helicopter takes to the skies over its home station at R.A.F. Odiham]

To the south of the village is R.A.F. Odiham, a front line support helicopter base and home of the R.A.F.'s heavy lift helicopter, the Chinook HC2. Squadrons 7, 18 (B) and 27 operate from Odiham, as does Army Air Corps

Squadron 657, which flies Lynx AH7s. The support helicopters provide essential transport of personnel and equipment at the battlefield, and are also used in support of R.A.F. ground units and as heavy-lift support for the Royal Marines.

Odiham had been a working airfield since 1925, but it was not officially opened as a permanent airbase until 1937, the ceremony being performed by the then Chief of Staff of the Luftwaffe, Erhard Milch. During World War II it had a dual role, both as a base for P-51 Mustangs and Hawker Typhoons and, after the allied invasion of Europe, as a prisoner of war camp.

In the mid 1950s the base was taken over by Transport Command, first operating Westland Whirlwind helicopters and then Bristol Belvederes, followed by the Westland Wessex in the 1960s and the Aérospatiale Puma in the 1970s.

The first Chinook was delivered in 1982, and Chinooks are very much in evidence in *Die Another Day*, since R.A.F. Odiham doubled as the United States bunker in the demilitarised zone in South Korea where Bond and Jinx are seen entering the helicopter hangar before descending to the bunker control room.

SOUTHAMPTON - SOUTHAMPTON DOCKS

Southampton Water is formed by the confluence of the Rivers Test and Itchen, with the Hamble joining it a little to the south. It is the ideal situation for a port. The area has been occupied, as archaeological finds show, since the Stone Age. Some time after AD70 the Romans chose it as the site of the stronghold called Clausentum, and in the 9th century frequent Viking raids spurred the Saxons to build the fortified settlement that became Southampton. By the 13th century Southampton was a leading port, particularly for the import of French wine and the export of English cloth and wool. The town was sacked in 1338 by French, Genoese and Monegasque ships under the command of Charles Grimaldi, who used the plunder to help establish the principality of Monaco. The following year King Edward III ordered an extensive rebuilding of the town defences, and around half the walling, thirteen towers and six gates still survive today. In the Middle Ages ship building became important, and the port has been used as a major military embarkation point from the Battle of Agincourt to World War II.

[The entrance to Southampton Docks is one of the few structures that have not been redeveloped since filming took place here in 1971]

The Southampton Docks Company was formed in 1835, the most famous departure, since the Mayflower in 1620, being RMS Titanic in 1912. Southampton became the home port for the Cunard company and later also the home of the flying boats of Imperial Airways. The port benefits from a sheltered location as well as unique double tides (which give seventeen hours a day of rising tides) making it the busiest cruise terminal and second largest container terminal in the United Kingdom. There are four terminals (Queen Elizabeth II, Mayflower, City and Ocean) with a new cruise terminal scheduled to open in 2013, which serve Cunard, P&O Cruises, Celebrity Cruises, Princess Cruises and Royal Caribbean, who between them have fourteen ships based in Southampton. The port also sees regular sailings from around fifty other cruise ships a year. On average one cruise ship a day visits the port.

It was on Ocean Terminal, before its redevelopment, that the James Bond production team descended for a day, July 15th 1971, to film Bond and Tiffany Case setting sail on their cruise in *Diamonds Are Forever*. In the film this is supposed to be Los Angeles docks. The ship they boarded was in fact the Canberra, then only ten years old, although the suite that is seen subsequently is just a Ken Adam film set. The Canberra was one of the most illustrious ships in the Cunard fleet, with a thirty-six year career, sailing more than three million miles and carrying nearly a million passengers. It was requisitioned for service in the Falklands campaign and underwent a two-day conversion in Southampton, in which a helicopter flight deck was put over the observation deck and swimming pool. The ship spent ninety-four days at sea, steamed more than twenty-five thousand miles, and landed most of the ground forces. When she returned to Southampton she was a sorry sight, streaked in rust. The Canberra then continued in service, being more popular than ever due to her military service, until 1997 when she was scrapped at Gadani Beach in Pakistan (a process that took nearly a year, rather than the estimated three months for a ship of her size, due entirely to her solid construction).

[Canberra in Southampton Docks in 1995]

Even for this rather simple sequence one hundred and fifty extras were used, along with a ton of streamers that the production crew had to clean up afterwards. Timing was also at a premium as the Canberra was on a quick turn around, which allowed only two hours for the actual filming.

Miscellaneous Locations

Beaulieu - National Motor Museum

[Palace House at Beaulieu]

In 1204 King John granted the Cistercian Monks the land on which to build the convent that would become known as Beaulieu Abbey. It was one of three monasteries founded by John, whose relations with the Order were strained, following his attempt to impose taxation on the Cistercians. He is thought to have established Beaulieu as a penance, after a nightmare of being flogged by monks. In 1204, thirty men came over from France to begin building, and by the end of the century nearly two hundred men lived and worked at Beaulieu.

Materials were brought from far and wide, to ensure that the structure was magnificent, as befitted a royal foundation. The abbey church, when complete, was three hundred and thirty-six feet long, and was reckoned to be the largest Cistercian church in England.

The abbey flourished for more than three hundred years, until England's religious houses were closed by King Henry VIII, their income appropriated by the King, and their assets sold or given to family or favoured subjects. This, the notorious 'dissolution of the monasteries', began in 1534. Beaulieu Abbey was dissolved in 1538, and the property, with its eight thousand acre estate, including the Beaulieu River, was acquired by Thomas Wriothesley, first Earl of Southampton, who paid £1,340 6s. 8d. for it. He demolished the church and many of the other buildings, but kept the lay brothers' quarters, the refectory, which he gave to Beaulieu village to be the parish church, and the great gatehouse, for his own use.

At first called Beaulieu Place, or Palace, what was originally a modest hunting lodge has long been known as Palace House. In 1709 the estate was inherited by John, 2nd Duke of Montague, who extended Palace House, building two wings around an open courtyard and adding a small tower at each corner. He also had a dry moat dug around the house, complete with a drawbridge, and it was he who created a garden by cultivating the surrounding fields.

During the last years of the 18th century the Beaulieu Estate passed into the family of the Dukes of Buccleuch. In 1867 the 5th Duke gave the Estate as a wedding present to his second son, Lord Henry Scott, grandfather of the present Lord Montagu: Beaulieu had its first resident owner.

The house is now home of Edward, 3rd Baron Montagu, who is happy to welcome Beaulieu's three hundred and fifty thousand annual visitors. All of the major rooms are open to visitors, including the most ancient rooms which were formerly part of the Great Gatehouse. On selected days, there are also tours of the private apartments.

In 1966 *A Man For All Seasons*, featuring Paul Scofield, Robert Shaw and Susannah York, was filmed on location on the Beaulieu River. In the same year, Palace House was also chosen as an outside location for *The Avengers*, starring Patrick Macnee and Diana Rigg. Margaret Rutherford came here to film *Stately Ghosts of England* in 1967 and sat up in the cloisters for several hours waiting for ghosts to appear – which of course they did not. Finally the 2005 film, *Mrs Palfrey at the Claremont*, starring Joan Plowright, was filmed in the Abbey Cloisters and outside Palace House.

However, for the James Bond enthusiast it is not Palace House but the National Motor Museum in the grounds that must be visited. The museum houses a collection of over two hundred and fifty automobiles and motorcycles, telling the story of motoring on the roads of Britain from the beginning to the present day. The displays vary from World Land Speed Record Breakers, including Campbell's famous *Bluebird* to film and television favourites including the 'Flying' Ford Anglia from *Harry Potter and the Chamber of Secrets*.

James Bond in Hampshire

[Instantly recognisable Bond vehicles at the *Bond in Motion* exhibition are the Aston Martin DB5 from *Goldfinger* (top) and the Lotus Esprit S1 from *The Spy Who Loved Me* (bottom)]

For many years there has always been at least one James Bond vehicle on display, and in 2012, for the fiftieth anniversary of the film series, there were no fewer than fifty on display for the *Bond in Motion* exhibition. This was the largest official collection of original Bond vehicles ever seen. Alongside the most famous machines, such as the Aston Martin DB5 and the Lotus Esprit S1, there is a host of treasures dating back to *From Russia With Love*, including the elegant Fairey Huntress Speedboat, Goldfinger's 1937 Rolls-Royce Phantom III, the buzzing autogyro from *You Only Live Twice* and the screeching Acrostar jet from *Octopussy*, alongside cars, bikes, trikes, sleds and boats.

118

James Bond in Hampshire

[Also present at the *Bond in Motion* exhibition are Auric Goldfinger's Rolls-Royce (top), along with the Acrostar jet (*Octopussy*) and 'Little Nellie' (*You Only Live Twice*) (bottom)]

For full details on Beaulieu please visit their website, www.beaulieu.co.uk. The Bond in Motion exhibition has been extended and will now run until the 5th January 2014

LEE-ON-THE-SOLENT - THE HOVERCRAFT MUSEUM

[No longer carrying the likes of James Bond, The Princess Margaret now resides at The Hovercraft Museum at Lee-on-the-Solent]

From its beginnings in 1988 The Hovercraft Museum has grown to a collection of sixty full-size craft, along with the largest hovercraft archive and library in the world. It has consolidated the collection on one waterfront site at Lee-on-the-Solent, the former home of various operational military hovercraft units from 1961 to 1982. A lot has been achieved, and the site has changed management from being an active Fleet Air Arm Navy Base (HMS Daedalus) to the current ownership by Gosport Borough Council.

2012 marks a special anniversary in the history of hovercraft. Fifty years ago, on the 20th July 1962, the world's first passenger hovercraft service was launched at the seaside resort of Rhyl in North Wales. The backdrop was the swinging 60s, and the hovercraft was an exciting and alluring new form of transport (and indeed James Bond travels from Dover (page 131) on *The Princess Margaret* in *Diamonds Are Forever*). The trial 'Hover Coach' service was operated by B.A.E., headed by the well-know airline entrepreneur Freddy Laker. The futuristic looking machine, which was described as sounding 'exactly like a four engined jet airliner', captured the public and media attention. This inaugural service saw the twenty-four seat craft flying passengers along a carefully chosen nineteen mile route to Moreton on the Wirral and back again for £2. Despite early promise, today the only scheduled passenger hovercraft service is from Southsea to Ryde on the Isle of Wight.

[Two of the Bond hovercraft on display at this unique museum]

However, this British invention is used throughout the world as a specialised transport in disaster relief, coastguard, military and survey applications, as well as for sport and some passenger services. In *Die Another Day* several specially adapted Osprey hovercraft, along with a Griffin 2000TD to represent Moon's hovercraft mothership, were used in filming the pre-title sequence at Aldershot and Chinnor (pages 105 and 143 respectively). The technical expertise of The Hovercraft Museum was very much involved in the filming. Three of the vehicles are currently on display at the museum.

The museum is normally only open by prior appointment, but there are also a few days a year when the site is allowed to open to the general public. Every year a full-blown Hovershow is staged to raise the funds necessary to cover the running costs, with around five thousand people visiting on such occasions. Regular work parties throughout each week carry out restoration and repair, archiving, hosting visits and other museum duties. The Hovercraft Museum is staffed entirely by volunteers. To find out more about the museum, its activities, and how to arrange a visit, please go to the museum website, www.hovercraft-museum.org.

PORTSMOUTH - PORTSMOUTH NAVAL BASE

Portsmouth Naval Base has been an integral part of the city since 1194. It is home to almost two-thirds of the Royal Navy's surface ships, including the aircraft carrier HMS Illustrious, new Formidable Type 45 destroyers, Type 23 frigates, and mine countermeasures and fishery protection squadrons. It will be home to two new aircraft carriers – HMS Queen Elizabeth and HMS Prince Of Wales – which are currently being built. At sixty-five thousand tonnes they will be the biggest ships ever built for the Royal Navy. The base is a major employer, with about sixteen thousand people working at peak times. It provides lodging facilities to Royal Navy personnel serving at the base and in Portsmouth-based ships.

In *Tomorrow Never Dies* there was a large naval presence in the form of HMS Chester, which is ordered by Admiral Roebuck to launch a missile into the terrorist arms bazaar during the pre-title sequence. Then later in the film HMS Devonshire is given false GPS information by one of Elliot Carver's satellites, causing her to stray into Vietnamese waters. The Devonshire is subsequently sunk by Carver's Dea Vac drill, launched from his stealth ship, but not before Carver has also shot down a Chinese MiG fighter, thus ensuring an international incident, especially when it transpires that the seventeen survivors have all been shot. As tensions mount, HMS Bedford is sent to the South China Sea just as Carver predicts. However, Carver is outwitted by Bond, who triggers an explosion aboard the stealth ship, damaging it and making it visible to the Bedford's radar. The British vessel pursues the stealth ship, which is ultimately destroyed when Stamper attempts to fire the stolen cruise missile, and at the very end of the film the Bedford is seen searching for Bond and Wai Lin among the wreckage – to no avail, for the two agents decide to stay 'under cover' just a little longer as the end titles roll.

[HMS Westminster, a Portsmouth-based Type 23 Frigate, doubled for all the Royal Navy ships seen in *Tomorrow Never Dies*]

All three ships were portrayed by HMS Westminster, a Type 23 frigate launched in 1992, with the exception of sequences where models were employed – as for example when Bond and Wai Lin explore the underwater wreck of the Devonshire. Understandably the Royal Navy were not too keen on sinking a real ship, even for a James Bond production! The filming all took place in the waters just off Portsmouth, Westminster's home port. HMS Westminster has been revamped and modernised on numerous occasions, and in 2004 she became Britain's first ship to receive the most advanced submarine-hunting sonar in the world, which, coupled with her Merlin helicopter, makes her a very potent threat to underwater foes.

[HMS Westminster docked at Portsmouth]

A visit to Portsmouth Historic Dockyard is worth a day of anybody's time. It is home to HMS Victory, The Mary Rose and HMS Warrior, as well as the National Museum of the Royal Navy. In addition there are harbour tours lasting around forty-five minutes where you may even come across HMS Westminster.

For more information see www.historicdockyard.co.uk.

JAMES BOND IN HERTFORDSHIRE
ABBOTS LANGLEY - LEAVESDEN STUDIOS

[Today Leavesden Studios is better known as the home of the Harry Potter films]

The Saxon settlement mentioned in the Domesday Book as Langlai was partly owned by the Abbot of St Albans and partly by the King, as may be seen in the names of Abbots Langley and Kings Langley. At the Reformation, King Henry VIII sold the Manor of Abbots Langley to Sir Richard Lee, and in 1641 Francis Combe left the manor in his will jointly to Sidney Sussex College, Cambridge and Trinity College, Oxford.

Abbots Langley's principal claim to fame is as the birthplace, in or about the year 1100, of Nicholas Breakspear, who, as Adrian IV, became the first and so far the only English Pope.

In 1866 streets were laid out on land between Abbots Langley and the neighbouring hamlet of Kitters Green, which had been bought by the British Land Company from the estate of one Sarah Smith. The names given to the new developments included Adrian Road, Breakspeare Road and Popes Road, in recognition of the village's famous son.

Leavesden Studios occupies the former aerodrome responsible for assembling and flight testing Wellington bombers, Halifax bombers, and Mosquito fighter-bombers during World War II. In 1966 the site was sold to Rolls-Royce for the production of aero-engines but closed in 1993.

Just as with Pinewood Studios (page 45) in the 1960s, it was EON Productions who came to the rescue, when in 1994 they were looking for facilities for filming the latest James Bond film, *Goldeneye*, and found Pinewood already committed to other filming. The old aircraft factory and airfield (two hundred and eighty-six acres in all) were ideal in terms of interior space (eight acres under one roof), privacy, a backlot (of eighty acres with, most importantly, a hundred and eighty degree uninterrupted horizon for exterior sets) and proximity to the industry-related services in the area.

In 1995, during the filming of *Goldeneye*, George Town Holdings acquired the site in order to develop filming, a business park, a residential complex and a studio tour. The next film, in 1996, was *Titanic* (1997), which was immediately followed by *Star Wars: Episode One – The Phantom Menace* (1999). Other productions such as *An Ideal Husband* (1999), *Sleepy Hollow* (1999) and *The Beach* (2000) followed, along with work for numerous commercials and music videos.

Today Leavesden Studios is one of only a few places in the United Kingdom where large scale productions can be made, and this no doubt was why, in 2000 and into 2001, Warner Bros. took over the entire complex for the filming of *Harry Potter and the Philosopher's Stone*. This was obviously a good move for the company, since every subsequent Harry Potter film was based here. Hence this truly is the home of Harry Potter on the big screen, especially since from June 2012 the site has also been home to the new Warner Bros. Studio Tour, which features authentic sets, costumes and props from the film series and showcases the British artistry, technology and talent that went into producing these iconic movies. However, none of this would have come about if it had not been for James Bond.

BOVINGDON - BOVINGDON AIRFIELD

The village of Bovingdon is around four miles south-west of Hemel Hempstead and has a population of some four thousand people. It is first recorded in 1200 as being Bovyndon, a probable corruption of Bufan dune, the Old English meaning 'above the down'.

Constructed in 1941-42, Bovingdon airfield was briefly home to No. 7 Group, R.A.F. Bomber Command, before being taken over in August 1942 by the U.S.A.A.F. 92nd Bombardment Group, which after flying two missions became a B-17 Flying Fortress Combat Crew Replacement Unit (CCRU). In January 1943, all the group except the 326th Bomb Squadron relocated to R.A.F. Alconbury, and the Eighth Air Force Headquarters and the Air Technical Section moved in to Bovingdon, along with General Eisenhower's personal B-17. The 11th CCRU was disbanded in September 1944, and Bovingdon became the base for the European Air Transport Service. The airfield was handed back to R.A.F. in 1947, and it was then taken over by the Ministry of Civil Aviation for civilian use. In 1951 the U.S.A.F. returned, and Bovingdon became the base for the 7531st Air Base Squadron, as well as housing the R.A.F. Fighter Command Communications Squadron. The Americans left in 1962, and R.A.F. Transport Command's Southern Communications Squadron operated from Bovingdon throughout the 1960s.

[It is not often that Bovingdon is mistaken for Bangkok, but this was the location for Scaramanga's flying car sequence in *The Man with the Golden Gun*]

The base closed in 1972, but, although military flights have ceased, the sky above is still busy, as a holding area for aircraft approaching Heathrow, known to pilots as the Bovingdon stack, and the airfield still houses a navigational radio beacon, code BNN.

Where the original aircraft hangers and administration block once stood is now part of The Mount Prison, an establishment for young male offenders, while the remainder of the site is occupied by a Saturday market and a paintballing company. Two of the three runways, along with the control tower, still exist albeit in a poor state of repair, while the other runway, taxiways and World War II bomb dump trackways have all been subject to hardcore reclamation, a common end to many disused airfields.

Close to the airfield is the Bobsleigh Inn on Box Lane, formerly the Bovingdon Country Club, which during World War II was where many celebrities, including Bob Hope, James Stewart and Glenn Miller, stayed while entertaining the troops at the base. The change of name honours the son of the owner, who at the 1964 winter Olympics at Innsbruck was half of the two man bobsleigh team that won a gold medal for Great Britain.

Bovingdon airfield should be quite familiar to the filmgoer, having made appearances in *The War Lover* (1962), *633 Squadron* (1964), *Mosquito Squadron* (1969) and *Hanover Street* (1979). It is also the airfield where Scaramanga's flying car takes to the air (not too realistically) in *The Man with the Golden Gun*.

JAMES BOND IN KENT

CHATHAM - THE HISTORIC DOCKYARD CHATHAM

["I'm looking for a submarine. It's big and black and the driver is a very good friend of mine", says Valentine Zukovsky, referring to his nephew as he confronts Elektra in *The World Is Not Enough*]

The name Chatham, first recorded in 880 as Cetham, probably derives from a pre-Saxon root indicating a settlement in a valley or river-basin. People have dwelt there since Roman times, as the town stands on the ancient road that the Saxons later named Watling Street, the route now followed by the main A2 from London to Dover. For centuries Chatham was no more than a quiet village beside the River Medway, but in the 16th century its strategic possibilities as a port were recognised, and warships were harboured there. It became a Royal Dockyard in 1569 during the reign of Queen Elizabeth I, initially just for repairs but then as a shipbuilding yard. Perhaps the most famous vessel launched here was HMS Victory, on the 7th May 1765 (although she did not leave Chatham for sea service until 1778). After World War I the dockyard concentrated on submarine building, with some fifty-seven being built between 1908 and 1960.

Around the dockyard various fortifications were built to defend the town from attack. Upnor Castle was built in 1567, but proved ineffectual when the Dutch made a raid on the Medway in 1667. This resulted in a whole complex of forts being constructed, including Fort Amherst which today is a major visitor attraction in the area. By the middle of the 19th century Chatham was surrounded by three rings of forts, including Fort Pitt (which shortly became a hospital and then the original home of the Army Medical School), Fort Luton, Fort Bridgewood and Fort Borstal. The soldiers and sailors who manned the forts were stationed at Kitchener Barracks, the Royal Marine Barracks, Brompton Artillery Barracks, Melville Barracks, and the naval barracks at HMS Collingwood and HMS Pembroke.

James Bond in Kent

Chatham's most famous resident was Charles Dickens, who later described his time there as the happiest years of his childhood. In 1856 he returned to the area, buying Gad's Hill Place in nearby Higham, where he lived until his death in 1870.

The whole area was a hive of activity until after World War II, when the importance of the dockyard began to decline. In 1984 it closed altogether with the loss of around seven thousand civilian jobs, representing almost a quarter of the town's adult population.

What now remains is a stunning eighty-acre site (out of an original four hundred acres) with historic buildings, museum galleries and historic warships, along with a vibrant programme of events and activities. The highlights include three historic warships (HMS Gannet, HMS Cavalier and the submarine HMS Ocelot), the Victorian ropery (a grade I listed building in which you can experience life as a rope maker and take a costumed guided tour), the wooden walls of England (an award-winning reconstruction of the dockyard of the Age of Sail), the historic lifeboat collection of seventeen vessels, and finally 3 Slip – The Big Space (containing such diverse exhibits as a Midget submarine, giant tools and steam machinery, Kitchener's railway carriage, the D-Day locomotive 'Overlord', mine-clearing equipment and a huge Chieftain tank). For further details see www.thedockyard.co.uk.

[Alongside the ropery building on the left is where a few seconds of the pre-title sequence in *The World Is Not Enough* was filmed, to show Bond taking his Q Boat under the left-hand archway and into the fish market]

The Kent Film Office makes great play of the fact that filming was done here for *The World Is Not Enough*, but the actual scene lasts just a few seconds, and purports to be London. During the pre-title boat chase, having gone through the boathouse at Tobacco Dock (covered in Volume 1), Bond then goes down an arched alleyway, through a fish market (supposedly Billingsgate) and through a restaurant, before emerging opposite the Millennium Dome. This sequence was filmed alongside the Victorian ropery.

Perhaps of more relevance is the submarine (see photograph on page 129), which stands between two of the historic ships. It is actually a remote control prop built for *The World Is Not Enough*, and based upon the Hotel Class of submarine used by the Russian navy between 1958 and 1964. For filming it was required to dive to over a hundred feet for the climax of the film, in which Bond kills Renard. These scenes were supposed to be in Istanbul, but were in fact done in the clearer water of the Bahamas. The exhibit is on loan from Turks Film Services Ltd., who are located within the dockyard complex.

Other productions filmed here include *The Golden Compass* (2007), *Amazing Grace* (2007), *The Mummy* (1999), *Sherlock Holmes* (2009) and *Les Miserables* (2012), while on the small screen *Foyle's War*, *Vanity Fair*, *Tipping the Velvet*, *Mill on the Floss*, *A Christmas Carol*, *Canterbury Tales* and most recently *Call The Midwife* and *Mr. Selfridge* have all been on location here.

DOVER - PORT OF DOVER FERRY TERMINAL

As Dover faces France across the narrowest part of the English Channel (just twenty-one miles to Cap Gris Nez) it will come as no surprise that the town has always been important as a port, and as a front line fortification against any enemies on the Continent. Archaeological finds have shown that there was a settlement here during the Stone Age, and that since the Bronze Age there was also a maritime connection. The Romans called the town Portus Dubris and built forts above the town along the chalk cliffs (commonly referred to as the White Cliffs of Dover), along with lighthouses to guide passing ships. The Domesday Book mentions Dover as an important borough, and, as if to underline this fact, it became one of the original Cinque Ports of Medieval England.

The town is in a valley through which the River Dour flows, making the original settlement an ideal port, sheltered from the prevailing south-westerly winds. In time the river mouth silted up so that today much of the town actually lies on reclaimed land. On one side is what is known as the Western Heights, while on the eastern side is Dover castle, a major tourist attraction with its museum and secret tunnels to explore.

["Mr. Franks, your passport is quite in order," Moneypenny tells Bond as he is about to board the hovercraft *en route* to Holland]

The town is dominated by the Port of Dover, which has been under the control of the Dover Harbour Board since 1606, during the reign of King James I. Despite a decline in traffic since the opening of the Channel Tunnel, the port still handles around sixteen million passengers and two million lorries annually. The busiest crossing is between Dover and Calais from the Eastern Docks with up to forty scheduled sailings every day. The Western Docks were always the more glamorous, being home to Admiralty Pier and its associated port facilities, the Golden Arrow cross-channel train services, hovercraft services, and the cruise terminal.

When *Diamonds are Forever* was filmed in 1971, the hovercraft service to France was seen as rather new and exciting, so naturally this was the only way for James Bond, under the name of Peter Franks, to travel on his way to Amsterdam. The hovercraft he boards is the *Princess Margaret*, built in 1968 by the British Hovercraft Corporation and retired in 2000. It is presently part of The Hovercraft Museum at former HMS Daedalus site at Lee-on-the-Solent (page 120).

James Bond in Kent

[This reminder of the hovercraft service is in town centre]

[The only remaining evidence of hovercraft operations]

It was a SR.N4 hovercraft, otherwise known as the Mountbatten class, and at the time the largest hovercraft in the world, having four Rolls-Royce Proteus marine turboshaft engines to carry two hundred and fifty passengers and thirty cars. The craft was forty metres long and weighed nearly two hundred tons, and was capable of a top speed of ninety-six miles an hour (although normally it would cruise at sixty-nine miles an hour). There was one tragic incident when in 1985 it was blown off course and into a breakwater at Dover, killing four passengers.

The first regular passenger service, from Dover to Boulogne, was officially inaugurated by Princess Margaret on the 1st August 1968. An operation to Calais began a year later, both services operating from the new Hoverport building in the Eastern Docks. However, as passenger numbers increased larger facilities were needed, and in 1978 a new terminal, costing £12 million, opened on fifteen acres of reclaimed land in the Western Docks. It remained the base for the cross-Channel hovercraft until the service closed entirely in 2005, having been rendered unprofitable by the abolition of duty-free. Today the site is deserted, with only one of the Rolls Royce turboshaft engines on display as a reminder of the glory days.

In *Diamonds Are Forever* we see Peter Franks, the diamond smuggler, arriving by car at passport control in the Eastern Docks, with the present passenger arrivals hall in the background. Informed that there is a message for him, he goes to park the car, and while the vehicle is out of shot Miss Moneypenny appears, dressed as an immigration officer. By the time she reaches the car, Bond has replaced Franks in the driving seat. To her remark that his passport is quite in order, he replies, "Well, anyone seeing you in that outfit, Moneypenny, would most certainly be discouraged from leaving the country." Asked what she would like him to bring her back from Holland, she says, "A diamond, in a ring." Bond's reply as he drives off towards the hoverport is, "Would you settle for a tulip?" The building still stands and has been refurbished, though it is no longer in use, and the surrounding area looks much as it did in the 1970s.

MANSTON - KENT INTERNATIONAL AIRPORT

[A scattering of aircraft at the underused Kent International Airport]

We know, from the discovery of some two hundred graves at what is now called the Ozengell burial ground, which has yielded both Roman and Anglo-Saxon artefacts, that Manston has been inhabited since ancient times. The name, originally Mannestone, probably indicates a farm at the top of a hill. The present spelling was in use by 1381, when the Peasants' Revolt reached the area. It was recorded: 'A proclamation in the name of Jack Straw and Wat Tyler ... called upon the people to destroy the Manston house of William de Medmenham, and if possible behead him'. Smugglers were active here in the 17th and 18th centuries, and in the two World Wars Manston became an important military air station.

The winter of 1915-1916 saw the open farmlands at Manston being used as a site of emergency landings, and as a consequence the Admiralty Aerodrome was opened. Initially it was a training school for Handley Page Type O bomber aeroplanes but by the end of 1916 the base also housed the Operational War Flight Command. In the Second World War it was a frontline airfield during the Battle of Britain. Hawker Typhoon and Meteor squadrons were stationed here, and it was from here that the bombers flew to test Barnes Wallis's bouncing bomb at nearby Reculver prior to the famous Dambusters raid in 1943. R.A.F. Manston was not only one of the closest airfields to occupied France but had one of the longest and broadest runways as well. Hence it was the designated airfield for any badly damaged aircraft who could not make it back to their own base. Consequently it became a graveyard for heavy bombers, which proved a valuable source of spares. Manston has two museums, the R.A.F. Manston History Museum and the Spitfire and Hurricane Memorial, both located at the northern edge of the airfield.

After the war and up until 1960 Manston came under the control of the Americans as a Strategic Air Command base, after which it reverted to R.A.F. control. It now became a base for training air cadets on De Havilland Chipmunks and for gliding activities. It was also at this time that the airfield saw some civilian passenger and cargo flights. In 1989 it became Kent International Airport, although officially the runway and other areas outside of the main thirty-five acre site still belonged to the R.A.F., who were legally responsible to maintain the runway, and provide air traffic control along with emergency fire and rescue services. Indeed, due to its length the runway (along with that at R.A.F. Fairford) was officially a designated emergency landing strip for the NASA Space Shuttle. In 1999 the remaining R.A.F. land was sold for housing development. The intention was that Manston would become a hub for budget airlines, but in 2005 the passenger side of the airport effectively went bankrupt with what was then London Manston Airport plc going into liquidation. Since then various other airlines have attempted to set up regular routes but to date none of them have seen the success they hoped for, and Manston remains in use mainly for charter work. The cargo side of the airport also went into administration in 2009, although the maintenance hangar is still use. The airfield still sees some activity for light aircraft and helicopter training.

No doubt it was the lengthy of the runway and the lack of scheduled aircraft movements that made Manston the ideal location for the North Korean airbase for the Antonov aeroplane sequence in *Die Another Day*. It took four days of night filming to complete, with Bond and Jinx breaking into the base while Graves, with high security, is having his cargo plane loaded with a helicopter and his supercars. As ever Bond, cannot just get onboard as everybody else would, so he and Jinx are seen running along the runway and entering via the landing gear as the aeroplane takes off.

JAMES BOND IN NORFOLK
BURNHAM DEEPDALE - DEEPDALE FARM

[Not an experimental car parking scheme for London but filming of *Die Another Day* at Deepdale Farm on the north Norfolk coast]

Along the Norfolk coast, between the striped cliffs of Hunstanton and the broad expanse of Stiffkey Marshes, are a dozen or so flint-walled villages, cut off from the sea by sand dunes and salt-marshes, which are constantly being reshaped as new land is won from the sea. The wildlife that thrives here on the marshes and creeks is protected by an almost continuous line of coastal nature reserves.

About halfway along this 20 mile stretch of coast, and connected to Brancaster Staithe by continuous buildings, is Burnham Deepdale, one of the 'Seven Burnhams' (the others being Burnham Norton, Overy, Sutton, Thorpe, Ulph, and Westgate). The most significant structure here is the round tower of the parish church, which is Norman in origin and built of flint soon after the Conquest. Inside is one of Norfolk's treasures – a medieval 'Seasonal Font', cut from a single block of stone and carved with twelve figures, each engaged in an activity appropriate to a month of the year, from drinking in January to feasting in December, by way of digging, weeding, mowing, and so forth.

137

The village centres upon the harbour and its thriving fishing and sailing community, and is known for its mussels in the winter. There are beautiful beaches and salt marshes alike, and wonderful views from Barrow Common which is popular for both painting and photography. Burnham Deepdale is also one of the driest villages in the country with always something to watch outdoors, be it a sky filled with pink-footed geese during the winter, or sailing, kiting, sea kayaking and other water sports during the summer.

Deepdale Farm, bordering Scolt Head Island nature reserve and with excellent views of the north Norfolk coast and access to marshland, has become a coastal film location for television productions such as *Dangerfield*, and *All the King's Men*. It is a working arable farm of some one thousand acres, growing wheat, barley, potatoes and sugar beet, although part of the area is flat land with water-filled ditches and springs. It is these ditches that double for paddy fields in North Korea in one of the final scenes of *Die Another Day*, in which Bond and Jinx, having just escaped by helicopter from Gustav Grave's cargo plane (fatally damaged after passing through the Icarus beam) fly off, passing a number of luxury cars (last seen in the hold of the disintegrating cargo plane and now miraculously undamaged) embedded in the mud. To create the effect took a reported thirty-five man crew and a whole month of preparation to transform part of the farm into the flooded paddy fields. This was achieved by building little walls to hold the water and then pumping water from the ditches to fill them. The actual filming took just one day with none of the main cast present.

Also well worth a visit and only two miles inland from here is Burnham Thorpe, famous as Nelson's birthplace. The old rectory where he was born in 1758 was pulled down in 1802, but All Saints' Church, isolated from the village, has the font where he was christened as well as a crucifix made of wood from HMS Victory, along with a bust of Nelson in the chancel.

MISCELLANEOUS LOCATION

SNETTERTON - SNETTERTON PARK MODELS

[The Soviet T55 tank used in *GoldenEye* now resides at Snetterton]

Snetterton is best known for its motor racing circuit, located at the former R.A.F. Snetterton Heath airfield. The base was designated a United States Army Air Force establishment and was only operational between 1943 and 1948. The circuit, just under 3 miles in length, is host to various races, including the British Touring Car Championship, British Formula Three Championship and the British Superbike Championship.

Part of the site is given over to a Sunday market, along with Snetterton Park Models, which claims to be the country's leading destination complex. Its seven halls are filled with displays and exhibits including toys, games, models, collectables, crafts, garden equipment and outdoor clothing. It is arguably the home of the largest toy exposition in the world. Outside there is a large picnic and play area for children, as well as a full size tank.

It is the tank that will be of interest to the James Bond enthusiast. It is based upon a Soviet T55 main battle tank, but made to look like a later T80

BV model, the one that features in *GoldenEye*. It is not a real tank, of course, but merely a fibreglass body fitted onto a Saladin armoured car chassis, which allowed it to be driven around the streets of St. Petersburg without causing any damage to the roads. Once it had finished its appearance in James Bond it was used by Sir Richard Branson to promote Virgin Cola. In the publicity stunt Sir Richard was seen driving the tank in Times Square, New York, and shooting at a Coca Cola sign.

The T55 dates from the very early 1960s and is a simple but robust tank that has seen service in many of the world's armed conflicts, right through to the 21st century. Indeed the T54/T55 series is the most produced tank in history with anything up to one hundred thousand produced for use in fifty countries. With its top speed of just over thirty miles an hour and a weight of thirty-six tonnes it is easy to see why the Russians preferred to have Bond drive the fibreglass version in the film.

JAMES BOND IN NORTHAMPTONSHIRE

SILVERSTONE - SILVERSTONE CIRCUIT

[The Hangar Straight, where according to Bond "some people on the roads really burn you up these days"]

The village of Silverstone is mentioned in the Domesday Book. During the Middle Ages the main trade was in timber felled from the surrounding Whittlewood Forest. The present parish church of Saint Michael was completed in 1884, although previous buildings for religious use have occupied the site since around 1200, and on the north side of the current churchyard the remains of some medieval fish ponds can be found.

Just to the south of the village is the former R.A.F. Silverstone, a World War II bomber base, which had three runways in a triangular format. These lie within the outline of the present Silverstone Circuit (which straddles the county boundary of Northamptonshire and Buckinghamshire), which was the idea of an *ad hoc* group of friends who in September 1947 set up an impromptu car race. Twelve drivers in all competed over a two mile circuit, during which one of the drivers ran over, and killed, a sheep that had wandered onto the disused airfield. With this in mind, the race was called the Mutton Grand Prix.

141

The following year the Royal Automobile Club took out a lease on the airfield and started to hold somewhat more formal races, making good use of the runways, which were connected by tight hairpin corners. In 1949 the perimeter track was used, and in 1952 the start line was moved from the Farm Straight to the straight linking Woodcote and Copse corners. This track configuration remained unaltered until 1975 when a chicane was introduced to curb the speeds through Woodcote Corner. Further remodelling of the circuit took place in 1987 and 1990 to make the circuit more technically challenging, albeit slower. Finally in 1995 the entry from the Hangar Straight into Stowe Corner was modified to make it less dangerous, and less demanding.

It is along the Hangar Straight in *Thunderball* that Fiona Volpe on her BSA motorcycle kills Count Lippe, sending his car skidding off the road into flames, while Bond in his Aston Martin observes the action in his rear view mirror, but for some reason does not give chase. The strangest thing, though, about this sequence, apart from the fact that there are no other cars present on the four-lane road, is that all three vehicles are driving on, and overtaking on, the wrong side of the road. Further, in the very next scene Volpe is seen discarding her motorcycle into a lake at Denham in Buckinghamshire (page 39), some sixty miles away.

Silverstone is the current home of the British Grand Prix, which it first hosted in 1948, the race in 1950 being the first in the newly-created Formula One World Championship. The race rotated between Silverstone, Aintree and Brands Hatch between 1955 and 1986, after which it was relocated permanently to Silverstone.

For more information about the Silverstone Circuit, race days and driving experiences see www.silverstone.co.uk.

JAMES BOND IN OXFORDSHIRE
CHINNOR - CHALK QUARRIES

[It is hard to imagine that this chalk pit could double as North Korea]

Chinnor lies at the foot of Chinnor Hill on the Icknield Way, and is one of the largest villages in Oxfordshire, with a population of around seven thousand people. There is archaeological evidence of a settlement here as early as the 4th century BC. However, the name, thought to mean the slope or incline of a man called Ceonna, is Anglo-Saxon. In time it became Chennore, then Chynor, and finally Chinnor. The Domesday Book records the village as belonging to a Saxon noble, but it passed into Norman hands soon after.

The village was a Roundhead troop station during the English Civil War. On the 18th June 1643 a Royalist force of nearly two thousand men led by Prince Rupert arrived from Oxford and overcame the Parliamentarians, taking one-hundred-and-twenty men prisoner. They were attacked on their way back to Oxford at Chalgrove Field but managed to fight off their pursuers. A few 16th and 17th century houses still remain, and many of the village's ghost stories and historical anecdotes date from this period.

Evidently Chinnor was a rough place to live in the late 18th century, when a petition signed by the local rector, along with thirteen tenant farmers, complained that there were so many alehouses that they were 'a check to

143

industry and good order' and called for one in particular, the Chequers, not to have its licence renewed. Apart from farming, the main industry, according to the 1851 census, was lace-making, which employed no less than two-hundred-and-sixty-eight persons, around of third of whom were children.

Chinnor station was opened in 1872 on the Watlington and Princes Risborough Railway, which in 1883 was taken over by the Great Western Railway. Sidings to the Chinnor cement works were added in 1927, and although the Beeching Axe ended passenger services in 1957, and freight services in 1961, the section between Princes Risborough and the cement works remained in operation until 1989. Fortunately the line was saved and from 1994 has been under the control of the Chinnor & Princes Risborough Railway, which runs steam trains on selected days throughout the year. The railway has appeared in *Midsomer Murders* and *Miss Marple*, and even hosts its own Sherlock Holmes mystery dinner trains.

The Chinnor Cement and Lime Company was founded in 1908, and became a public concern in 1936. It established a quarry in the Chiltern escarpment south of the village, along with a cement works. By 1975 it employed one-hundred-and-sixty persons and had plans to double in size. At its peak the quarry manufactured 5,600 tonnes of cement a week. However, the works closed in 1989 and the cement works, whose chimneys once were a landmark, and somewhat of an eyesore, in this beautiful area, were demolished in 2010-11. Interestingly the works would have closed sooner it were not for an increased demand for cement for the Channel Tunnel, under construction at the time. In fact one of the boring machines for the tunnel was first tested here.

There area has since been redeveloped and now forms part of a housing estate, although the striking chalk pit lakes remain and have been used for filming, posing as a far away state in the television series *Ultimate Force*.

In 2002 the James Bond production team filmed the final stage of the pre-title sequence for *Die Another Day* in the chalk pits. The initial part of the hovercraft chase sequence was done in Hampshire at the Eelmoor Driver Training Area (page 106) but the scene in which Bond is 'saved by the bell' after Colonel Moon's hovercraft crashes through a gate and plunges down a waterfall, and Bond is subsequently captured by North Korean soldiers and imprisoned by Moon's father, General Moon, was shot at Chinnor, as the clearly visible chalk deposits attest.

FINMERE - FINMERE AIRPORT

[It seems appropriate that the location where Bond's aeroplane crashes in *You Only Live Twice* now a centre for Micro-Flights]

Finmere is right on the border with Buckinghamshire, only 4 miles from Buckingham itself. Archaeological evidence suggests human activity here during the Bronze Age, Iron Age and Roman times. Indeed the line of former A421 and Mere Lane is along that of the original Roman road from Alchester to Towcester, and Bronze Age ring ditches, which surrounded burial mounds, have been found in the gravel quarry at Foxley Fields. The name of the village is derived from the Old English for 'pond frequented by woodpeckers' or 'boggy area with a pond'.

After the Norman Conquest the estate was split between the Bishop of Coutances and the Bishop of Bayeux. The manor subsequently passed first to the Earls of Gloucester, and later to the Earls of Stafford. During the reign of King Henry VIII Finmere became his personal possession and was given in turn to four of his Queens (Catherine of Aragon in 1509, Jane Seymour in 1536, Anne of Cleeves in 1540 and Catherine Howard in 1541). In 1602 the Temple family first bought land in the area, and by 1753 they owned most of the parish. In 1822 Richard Temple was made the Duke of Buckingham and Chandos. This was the same Temple family who owned Stowe (page 69) from where the village was administered. During the Civil War there was a minor skirmish in Finmere when a force of twenty Parliamentarian troops, under Captain Andrewes, surprised a troop of eighteen Royalist soldiers who were stationed in the village. The retreating Cavaliers were captured at nearby Fringford, and Finmere came under Cromwell's control. When the fortunes of the Temple family declined some of the parish was sold to Merton College, Oxford.

During World War II R.A.F. Finmere was constructed just south of the village and became operational in July 1942. It was never a front line station being used as a satellite to nearby R.A.F. Bicester, and as an operational training unit, flying Bristol Blenheim medium range bombers, which were by then considered obsolete for combat. In 1944 these were replaced by de Havilland Mosquitoes, and the base became a major centre for turning out fully trained aircrew for the war effort in the Far East. After the war the airfield became a storage depot before being closed altogether in the 1950s. This is where the aeroplane crash and parachute scene in *You Only Live Twice* was filmed. Helga Brandt and Bond are travelling in a Cessna aeroplane, escaping SPECTRE, somewhere over Japan. However, the fields below are in fact those of Tingewick and Finmere, with Brandt bailing out over Finmere, and Bond crash-landing on the remaining main east-west runway of the former R.A.F. base, which is today used for microlight flights and training.

Oxford - Brasenose College
New College

[Brasenose College where you can brush up on a little Danish]

The College takes its name from the bronze sanctuary knocker, first recorded in a document of 1279, which used to be attached to the main gate of the Brasenose Hall. The importance of the knocker was that colleges, like churches, were regarded as sanctuaries and so any fugitives were safe from the authorities once they had clutched the knocker. It was removed to Stamford in the 1330s, since Oxford was considered at that time to be too turbulent a place. In 1890 it was brought back to Oxford and has hung ever since in the hall, over high table. Over the centuries many halls have occupied the site which today is Brasenose College. These included Burwaldescote (1247-1469), Amsterdam, St. Thomas's Hall (formerly Staple Hall), Sheld Hall, Ivy Hall, Little University Hall, Salysbury Hall and Little Edmund Hall.

Brasenose College was founded in 1509 by William Smyth, Bishop of Lincoln, and Richard Sutton, a successful lawyer. Since at this time the original knocker was at Stamford a new brazen nose was produced which contains the caricature of a human face. This knocker is presently located at the apex of the main gate, while stained-glass representations may be found in the northern oriel window in the hall, alongside portraits of the two founders. The college coat of arms consists of devices of the founders and the diocese of Lincoln, and is one of only three known examples of tierced arms in England, the others belonging to Lincoln and Corpus Christi Colleges.

The college prospered due to the generosity of the early benefactors, though there was discontent among the Junior Fellows, who considered their income too low in comparison to the Senior Fellows and the Principal. It was not without financial scandal, to the extent that in 1643 some Fellows petitioned King Charles I to institute a Visitation. Most of these abuses flourished under the autocratic rule of Principal Radcliffe (1614-48). However, despite these setbacks the college expanded to twenty-one Fellows from the original twelve. Probably the most famous Principal of the 16th century was Alexander Nowell, who is also credited with the invention of bottled beer.

After the Civil War in 1647 the College was in debt again and experienced a Parliamentary Visitation. Principal Radcliffe was ousted and Daniel Greenwood appointed in his place. He was largely responsible for turning the college finances around and ensuring the stability of Brasenose for the next century, during which time the college became firmly Jacobite. Whereas the 18th century saw Brasenose as a place of intellectual distinction, the 19th century saw it acquire a new reputation for sporting achievements, particularly in rowing and cricket.

Among the notables of Brasenose College are Sir Charles Holmes (director of the National Gallery from 1916-28), John Buchan, Field-Marshal Earl Haig, Lord Scarman, Robert Runcie (former Archbishop of Canterbury) and John Mortimer. Today the College has forty Fellows, twenty-three lecturers, ninety-two graduates and three hundred and twenty-nine undergraduates. Since 1974 it has been co-residential. As far as James Bond is concerned, another student of Brasenose from 1931 should also be included in this list, Paul Dehn, who won an Oscar in 1951 for Best Story (now called Best Original Screenplay) for *Seven Days to Noon*, and missed out on another for *Murder on the Orient Express*. Harry Saltzmann brought him in to write a second draft for *Goldfinger* in 1963 when the original script by Richard Maibaum was described as being 'very English now and then, coy, arch, self-consciously tongue-in-cheek'. Dehn was responsible for such lines as "I have a slight inferiority complex" (when asked why he always wears a gun), and most famous of all "Do you expect me to talk ... No, Mr. Bond. I expect you to die"- maybe one of the most famous exchanges in film history.

The college makes a brief appearance in *Tomorrow Never Dies*, as the interior shots of Professor Inga Bergstrom's room, where she is teaching Bond Danish, were filmed here.

Until 1400 New College was known as the College of St. Mary of Winchester in Oxford, but changed its name to distinguish it from the other St. Mary's College, which later became Oriel College. Originally it was one of the six theology colleges, and by far the largest, principally for those entering the clergy, with only those scholars from Winchester being eligible to become college Fellows. New College was the first to be based around a quadrangle that contained all the major buildings. The construction was overseen by the founder, William of Wykeham, Bishop of Winchester, who also was also responsible for the building of the royal lodgings at Windsor Castle. He was a shrewd businessman as well, buying the land cheaply as it had been the City Ditch, used for burials at the time of the Black Death, and said to be 'full of filth, dirt and stinking carcasses'. The foundation stone was laid on 5th March 1380, and the buildings erected in increments between then and 1403, when the bell-tower was completed.

One of the most interesting buildings is the chapel, which is T-shaped, with an antechapel at right-angles to the nave. This allowed for worship in the nave while private Masses could be conducted in the antechapel, where disputations and elections were also held. The chapel was built in the

Perpendicular style, though decoration was restrained. The original roof was probably a tiebeam construction, but today a taller hammerbeam roof designed by Sir George Gilbert Scott survives, along with sixty-two of the original misericords in the Fellows' stalls, many of which show rich images of Oxford life, from a doctor lecturing, to scholars fighting with daggers. The rest of the wooden features and the figures on the reredos belong firmly in the Victorian era.

[The Holywell Quadrangle at New College provides a suitable parking spot for Bond in Oxford]

In 1528 the Protestant Reformation was felt in the College when the then Warden, Dr. London, deprived John Quinbey of his Fellowship on account of his heresy. He was subsequently imprisoned in the bell-tower where he starved to death. While obeying the commands of King Henry VIII, which included the destruction of many of the college's precious manuscripts, the college remained a centre for the Catholic faith, which was to continue until Queen Elizabeth I purged many of the Catholic Fellows. In addition the chapel altar was removed, much of the Medieval glass destroyed, and the reredos plastered over. As a result the college was no longer seen as being at the forefront of religious leadership in Oxford.

However, New College continued to grow in size, and even the Civil War did little to change the place, despite the cloisters acting as the main arsenal for the king's army, following the defeat at Edgehill in 1642. Cromwell did have fifty of the Fellows ejected, to be replaced by fifty-five new Fellows along with a new Warden, George Marshall, a Cambridge man. This regime was short-lived, for during the Restoration the college was again to thrive, with the expulsion and appointment of yet more Fellows. Indeed, New College became the richest in revenues save for the colleges of Christ Church and Magdalen, although academically, with Fellowships being bought and sold, standards fell and the college became more of a club where Fellows were 'much given to drinking and gaming and vain brutish pleasure' and where 'they degenerate in learning'.

There was at this time much building and redesigning taking place, nowhere more than in the chapel. Between 1736 and 1740 William Price of Hatton Garden restored the windows on the south side of the nave, and in 1765 William Peckitt of York repaired the north side and west window (the removed glass actually being sold to York Minster, where it remains to this day). The Fellows disliked the new west window so much that in 1777 they had the glass moved to a window in the north-east of the nave, and commissioned Joshua Reynolds to design another west window, depicting the Nativity.

Further, between 1789 and 1794 James Wyatt made a plaster vault in the roof and replaced the reredos with plaster imitations of the originals (though these were in turn replaced during the Victorian era by ones in stone, whose niches were filled with sculptures by J. L. Pearson).

With refurbished buildings came more rigorous academic standards and a consequent rise in undergraduates from 1810, though for many years the college preserved its right of exempting its members from the University examinations. It was not until 1857 that various reforms were agreed upon, which (along with others over the next thirty years) brought the college into line with the rest of the university. Today the college is particularly strong in the sciences, though it is interesting to note that female students were not admitted until 1979.

The original main (west) entrance to the college was via New College Lane (as opposed to Holywell Street) which runs from Catte Street under the bridge of Hertford College to Queen's Lane. It would seem that finding a place to leave his car in Oxford is a problem even for Bond, since the establishing shot of his parked Aston Martin DB5 in *Tomorrow Never Dies* is just inside the Holywell Street entrance of New College. This might seem strange given that he was undertaking his Danish lessons at Brasenose College some distance away, but then it must be remembered that Bond is not that familiar with Oxford, having obtained a first in Oriental languages at Cambridge (as Bond informs Moneypenny in *You Only Live Twice*). In the books Bond would be even less familiar with both establishments, having gone straight from Fettes College in Edinburgh to the University of Geneva, where, like Ian Fleming, he stayed only briefly.

STONOR - STONOR PARK
WHITEPOND FARM

[Stonor Park is not a safe, safe house in *The Living Daylights*]

The village of Stonor may seem old but in fact it only came into existence in 1896, when the parish of Upper Assendon was divided, and Stonor was named after the adjacent country house, Stonor Park. The village was remarkable during the English Reformation in that the Stonor family, along with many of the local gentry, were recusants. In 1581 the Jesuit priests Edmund Campion and Robert Parsons lived and worked at Stonor Park, and on the 4th August 1581 a raid on the house uncovered a press on which Roman Catholic literature had been secretly printed. The literature in question was a pamphlet which described the 'ten reasons why the historical Catholic faith should be preferred over the teachings of the newly Established Church'. Although Campion (who was to be martyred in 1581) and Parsons had left the house a few days earlier, the elderly Lady Cecily Stonor, her son, the Jesuit priest William Hartley, the printers and four servants were all arrested, and Hartley was later exciled. During the 17th and 18th centuries the Stonors, along with a number of locals, were fined and prosecuted many times, but remained of the Roman Catholic faith throughout, using the private chapel at Stonor Park for their worship. The Stonors also endowed the local school, which was Roman Catholic, and in so doing ensured that this community remained of that faith for many generations.

The house at Stonor Park is built on the site of a prehistoric stone circle, one stone of which is incorporated into the south-east corner of the private Chapel of the Holy Trinity, which is otherwise constructed of flint with an early brick tower. The other stones from the circle are a mixture of sarcens, block of sandstone, and puddingstones, pebbles stuck together by natural limestone cement that has washed between them and hardened into solid rock. Unfortunately they were not left in their original positions and were re-positioned during the 17th century landscaping of the grounds, and the 20th century reconstruction, and hence are classed as a folly, rather than an ancient monument, such as Stonehenge. The positioning of the stone in the chapel follows the teaching of Pope Gregory the Great, who in 601 instructed the missionary priests in England to adopt existing religious sites of worship as their own. The most recent repair work to the chapel was carried out in the 1950s by the 6th Lord Camoys, the Stations of the Cross, which were carved by Jozef Janas, a Polish prisoner or war in World War II, being a gift from the author, Graham Greene in 1956.

It is thought that the house was begun after 1280, when Sir Richard Stonor married his second wife, Margaret Hamhull. It is basically an E-shaped Tudor manor house, but with a red brick façade and Georgian windows. However, looks can be deceptive, since behind the exterior is a much older collection of buildings, including a medieval hall, a 17th century library with a magnificent vaulted ceiling and containing an important collection of recusant literature. Today visitors may visit the public rooms, which contain some fine furniture, family portraits, bronzes, stained glass, silhouettes, Italian pictures and drawings and a growing collection of contemporary ceramics, as well as the room, roof space and priest hole occupied by Campion and his colleagues. The house and gardens are generally only open on Sundays between March and September, as well as Bank Holidays and Wednesdays in July and August. For further details please see www.stonor.com.

[The way to the kitchens as used by Necros]

Stonor Park can be spotted on the television in *Hornblower* and *Midsomer Murders*, as well as in the television movie *Danny the Champion of the World* (1989).

Perhaps because of its secret past it was also the location chosen as Bladen's safe house, where the defecting Koskov is taken in *The Living Daylights*. Bond is seen arriving in his Aston Martin, with a hamper for Koskov, and joins the debriefing inside. All the interior shots were in fact done back at Pinewood Studios. Next Necros, disguised as a milkman, arrives in his milk float and is directed to the kitchen via the tradesmen's entrance. He is then seen passing through the large wooden gates to the left of the main house.

On screen the explosions that subsequently take place as a result of Necros' exploding milk bottles seem real enough, and for good reason, since they are real. This must be one of the few occasions that actual explosions were allowed inside such a historic property, though the effect was achieved under carefully controlled conditions with the original Georgian windows replaced by props. There are further establishing shots of the house and grounds as the helicopter arrives to complete Koskov's capture.

[White Pond farm, where you should always beware of joggers]

The action prior to this sequence took place just north of the village itself in Balham's Lane. This is where Necros is first seen jogging past the milk float that is delivering to White Pond Farm. As the unlucky milkman returns to his float, Necros appears from behind the farm's garden wall and strangles him with the cord of his headphones, before requisitioning his vehicle and introducing his own explosive version of gold top.

UPPER HEYFORD - R.A.F. UPPER HEYFORD

[The entrance to Feldstadt Air Base in *Octopussy* is just a prop constructed along Offut Drive at R.A.F. Upper Heyford]

Upper Heyford stands on the east bank of the River Cherwell, approximately 6 miles north-east of Bicester and close to the Oxford Canal. It is named as Haliford in the Domesday Book, at which time it was owned by the Norman baron Robert D'Oyly, whose tenants, the de Chesney family, ran the estate until the late 12th century. After several changes of owner, the manor was bought for £1,000 in 1380 by William of Wykeham, Bishop of Winchester, who granted it to his newly founded New College, Oxford (page 148), which has retained it ever since.

Today the village comprises just over one hundred homes in all styles, with some of the more picturesque buildings dating from the 18th-19th century and constructed of Cotswold stone. Around a mile to the east of the village is the former R.A.F. Upper Heyford, which is now a substantial industrial and commercial estate.

The base was first used by the Royal Flying Corps in 1916 but was not brought into use for flying until 1918. Throughout its life, right up to 1950, it was mainly used as a training facility (including parachute training), while during the Cold War it became a United States Air Force Strategic Air Command base for bombers, and later tactical reconnaissance, fighter and fighter-bomber aircraft. During this time the site boasted the second longest runway in Europe, which was needed for the B-36s and B-50s that were stationed here. In September 1952 the base had a full complement of forty-five aircraft, and in 1965 special operations were transferred there from nearby Brize Norton, which had been returned to the R.A.F. Upper Heyford was very much in the news in 1982, when a peace camp was established by a group of protestors who wished to highlight the fact that the base had F-111 aircraft armed with nuclear weapons on fast response. The camp lasted for two years, and during one demonstration in 1983 some four thousand people took part over a four day period, with the police making seven-hundred-and-fifty-two arrests.

With the ending of the Cold War activity at the base was gradually scaled down, with the final flight taking place on 15th December 1993 and the base being returned to the Ministry of Defence on the 30th September the following year. The runways are now home to a variety of wildlife including peregrine falcons, skylarks and buzzards, and the site as a whole is home to a number of activities, from a car storage pound, to police driver training and narrow boat building. However, much of the base is still boarded up and it is uncertain what the future will bring. There have been several redevelopment proposals, mainly for new housing (up to ten thousand properties), which have to date all been rejected.

The base does make a good film set and has been used in *The Fourth Protocol* (1987) with among other a young Pierce Brosnan in a plot not too dissimilar to that of *Octopussy*, and *World War Z* (2013) with Brad Pitt. It has also featured in the television series *Lewis*.

[The crest of the U.S.A.F. $20^{th}/120^{th}$ T.F.W.]

However, by far the most prominent filming to take place here was for *Octopussy*, in which Upper Heyford was transformed into Felstadt Air Base, a United States Air Force base in West Germany. The transformation involved the addition of a brick wall to gate one, a pitched roof to the gate's guardhouse, an entrance in Offutt Drive and a circus tent in front of hangar three. In addition the 20th Tactical Fighter Wing was re-designated the 120th.

Two scenes were filmed over the period of a week. The first involved the circus parade down Offut Drive and through gate one, complete with majorettes, band and circus animals. The second is that of Bond arriving at the base, pursued by the German police. The chase begins in Camp Road and ends at gate one, as Bond asks to see the base commander.

[Two scenes from the circus parade with crowds composed of Upper Heyford military personnel and their families – around two hundred people were allowed to participate]

James Bond in Oxfordshire

[Preparation and attention to detail, as demonstrated with the above signs, is paramount in filming a feature such as *Octopussy*. The crest used for the 120th Tactical Fighter Wing is in fact borrowed from the 20th Tactical Fighter Wing. The two men in the bottom picture have just completed building the brick wall and pillar which Bond will later demolish as he crashes through the barrier at gate one]

158

James Bond in Oxfordshire

[Gate No. 1 as it was during filming (top) and as it is today (bottom). Note the extension to the guard house and new security fence]

James Bond in Oxfordshire

[In the chase sequence Bond approaches the guard house (top) and asks for the base commander (bottom). Note the rear car loading]

160

James Bond in Oxfordshire

[Bond crashes through the chain barrier (top) and drives off with the guard firing into the air (bottom). Note that for this shot the top of the pillar, which was constructed with a section designed to drop off as Bond crashes through the chain barrier, has been replaced in the bottom picture. It was so this minor stunt could be performed successfully that the rear of the car was loaded. Also note that although the actors and extras are in the same position for each take the car and the aeroplane to the right have both moved from their original alignment. Finally the 'UH' markings on the tails of the F-111s gives a large indication that this is Upper Heyford and not somewhere in West Germany, plus the fact that Bond is driving on the left]

161

[Finally the police arrive in hot pursuit (top) while Roger Moore, looking relaxed and with cigar, observes the shooting from a position of safety]

[Today the site where Octopussy's Circus big top once stood is still very recognisable but sadly abandoned]

MISCELLANEOUS LOCATIONS

DRAYTON ST. LEONARD - ASTON MARTIN HERITAGE TRUST

[The great tithe barn at Drayton St. Leonard now houses the Aston Martin Heritage Trust museum and archive]

The village of Drayton St. Leonard is situated on the River Thame around 8 miles southeast of Oxford. At the time of the Domesday Book it was part of Dorchester-on-Thames, then owned by the Bishop of Lincoln, and remained with the estate after Dorchester Abbey was dissolved by King Henry VIII in the 1530s. By the 18th century the major landowner was the Earl of Abingdon, and in the 19th century Trinity College, Oxford acquired property in Drayton. The oldest parts of the parish church of St. Leonard and St. Catherine, originally a chapel of the Peculiar of Dorchester, are the Norman doorways in the north and south walls, dating from 1146. A stained glass window of the mid 14th century portrays St. Leonard, but most of the present stained glass dates from the 1859 restoration. The ring of six bells was cast at the famous Whitechapel Bell Foundry in 1884. The village consists of nearly one hundred properties, around fifteen of them dating from the 16th and 17th centuries.

Built in the 15th century by the monks of Dorchester Abbey, the great tithe barn at Drayton St. Leonard now houses the Aston Martin Heritage Trust museum and archives and also acts as headquarters for the Aston Martin Owners Club.

The Trust was established in 1998 by the Club, partly to provide a safe haven for its heritage collection of assets and partly to create an organisation dedicated solely to preserving and enhancing the history of Aston Martin. Since then, the trust has very significantly enhanced the collection.

Among the highlights on view are an A3, the oldest known Aston Martin in existence, a 1933 Ulster, one of only twenty-nine in existence, and the prototype AMR1/01 that came 11th in the 1988 Le Mans 24 hour race. The museum also houses a fascinating and varied collection of artefacts including photographs, documents and objects from Aston Martin Lagonda Ltd. and the Aston Martin Owners Club.

The museum is open to the public, but is not set up for large numbers of visitors, so please contact the Aston Martin Heritage Trust in advance and make an appointment if you intend to visit (www.amht.org.uk) and remember that the museum is aimed primarily at the serious Aston Martin enthusiast.

NETTLEBED - JOYCE GROVE

Nettlebed lies on the Henley-on-Thames to Oxford road, and was an important stop-over for stage coaches in bygone days. Many members of royalty are rumoured to have stayed at the former Red Lion public house in the High Street. However, this interesting village is most famous for having an abundance of clay suitable for brick making. In the 13th century there was even a settlement of Flemish bricklayers in nearby Crocker End. One of the listed buildings in Nettlebed is a late 17th century brick kiln, later adapted for burning lime. Unused since 1938, it was restored in 1975 with the support of local people and Oxfordshire County Council.

The name of the village may derive from the fact that thread can be obtained from nettles and woven into linen cloth. In the 18th century many homes had bed linen and tablecloths made from, nettles that are found in abundance in the area. The White Hart Hotel in the High Street, originally called The George, adopted its present name in the reign if Henry VIII, probably to reflect the King's passion for hunting deer. A century later, during the Civil War, Royalist troops were billeted here, and King Charles himself may have visited the inn.

["Oh, and I suppose that's completely inconspicuous," as M might have commented when the publisher visited Joyce Grove in an appropriate car]

Nettlebed owes its connection with James Bond, or rather, his creator, to the large Grade II listed house called Joyce Grove, which stands in extensive grounds behind the High Street. The house was built in 1903 by Ian Fleming's grandfather, Robert Fleming, who, six years later, was to found the merchant bank that bears his name. Having bought two thousand acres of land and many properties in the village, Fleming had his new mansion constructed of red brick with Bath stone dressing, in the Jacobean style. In 1940 his elder grandson Peter Fleming gave the house to St. Mary's Hospital, Paddington for a convalescent home, a role it fulfilled for more than thirty years, before becoming a Sue Ryder hospice in 1979. At the time of writing, the charity plans to move to a new site in Henley-on-Thames, and Joyce Grove is to be sold some time in 2013. The house has been seen on screen in *Jeeves and Wooster* as Deverill Hall, and in *Midsomer Murders* as Bledlow Manor.

Ian Fleming was the banker's younger grandson. Until the success of the James Bond books, the really famous member of the family was Ian's elder brother Peter Fleming, renowned as a journalist and travel writer. In 1935 he married the actress Celia Johnson, today best remembered for the film *Brief Encounter*. Members of the Fleming family still live in Nettlebed, running the Joyce Grove estate and taking an active part in village life. Among the family graves in the parish churchyard are those of Peter Fleming and his wife Dame Celia Johnson.

The grounds are open to the public only on when fetes are held to raise money for the care home. These tend to take place around one a month during the summer.

JAMES BOND IN SUFFOLK
ELVEDEN - ELVEDEN HALL

[The Italian inspired exterior of Elveden Hall gives no clues as to the exotic interior used in *The Living Daylights*]

In a Latin text of the mid-twelfth century Elveden is called *vallis nympharum*, valley of the nymphs, supporting the notion that the English name derives from the Old English for elves' valley. Today this village of under three hundred persons is known for three things. First it appears regularly on traffic reports, since the traffic lights at the crossroads with the main A11 between Cambridge and Norwich are a particular bottleneck in the area, causing long queues. Second Elveden Forest is home to a large Centre Parcs resort, which acts as a major employer in the area, and finally there is the 10,000 acre Elveden Estate, the centrepiece of which is Elveden Hall.

Upon the dissolution of the monasteries, the Estate, formerly in the possession of Bury Abbey, was given by King Henry VIII to the Duke of Norfolk. The core of the present house, built in the 1760s for Admiral Keppel, is incorporated in the west wing, designed in 1879 by John Norton for Prince Duleep Singh.

[The interior of Elveden Hall easily doubled for Tangier where Bond shoots blanks at Pushkin from the balcony on the right hand side of the picture]

In 1854, Duleep Singh, Maharajah of the Punjab and owner of the Koh-i-noor diamond, was exiled to Britain, having been deposed in 1849 by the East India Company, who promptly annexed his kingdom. The famous diamond was given to Queen Victoria, and Duleep Singh received a pension of £50,000 a year. In 1863 he bought the Elveden Estate, all 17,000 acres, and had John Norton rebuild the Hall in the Italian style. The interior, however, was made to resemble a Mughal palace, and an aviary, stocked with exotic birds, was constructed outside.

Being particularly fond of the sport, the Maharajah often held shooting parties at Elveden, in which many members of the aristocracy took part. Sadly, during the 1870s there were several bad years for the crops, his personal fortunes declined, and political tensions increased. He left England in 1886 and died seven years later in Paris. The estate was sold to the 1st Earl of Iveagh, Edward Cecil Guinness of the brewing dynasty, whose family still owns it. The Hall suffered severe damage during World War II, and the entire contents were sold at auction in 1984.

Thanks, no doubt, to its unique architecture the hall has appeared in a number of film productions including *The Moonstone* (1997), *Eyes Wide Shut* (1999), *Lara Croft: Tomb Raider* (2001), *Stardust* (2007) and *Dean Spanley* (2008).

The exotic foreign interiors doubled for those to be found in Tangier for a key sequence in *The Living Daylights* involving the assassination of Pushkin faked by Bond in order to trap Koskov. At the time of filming, in 1987, the house was empty, making it easier for the production company to move in for just the couple of days that were required to complete this scene.

Although the house is private there are some parts of the estate that are open to the public (see www.elveden.com for full details).

LAKENHEATH - R.A.F. LAKENHEATH

Lakenheath stands where Fenland meets Breckland, close to the border with both Norfolk and Cambridgeshire. The fens are low-lying marshy flatlands, with small scattered hills or 'islands', most notably the Isle of Ely. Since the 17th century the area has been successively drained by wind, steam, electric and diesel pumps to reveal an abundance of rich, peaty farmland. The whole area is covered in a network of long straight waterways, from the size of ditches to large rivers. Lakenheath High Street itself is only ten metres above sea level, while other parts of the parish are actually at sea level. In 1996 Lakenheath Fen Nature Reserve turned heavily farmed fields back to reed beds and grazing marshes. Cranes are now breeding there for the first time since the 16th century. Breckland is a low chalk plateau with sandy soil, beneath which have been found tools dating back half a million years, proving that the area has been inhabited since the Old Stone Age. Much of the area remains gorse-covered heath, despite the creation in 1914 of the twenty-three thousand acre Thetford Forest.

The most remarkable building in the town is the church, Saint Mary's, built of flint. Inside are medieval paintings and medieval carvings on the pews. The faces of the wooden angels were all damaged in the Civil War by the religiously motivated puritan soldiers. Among the paintings are those depicting St. Edmund, angels and birds, all from the 13th century and currently under restoration thanks chiefly to a grant from the Heritage Lottery Fund.

[An F-15 taxis at the United States Air Force base in the South China Sea, actually R.A.F. Lakenheath]

However, today by far the most important feature of the area is R.A.F. Lakenheath, which hosts the largest United States Air Force Base in the country and is home to the 48th Fighter Wing, known as the Statue of Liberty Wing. There are over five thousand active-duty personnel supporting three combat-ready squadrons of F-15E Strike Eagle and F-15C Eagle fighter aircraft, along with HH-60G helicopters belonging to the 56th Rescue Squadron.

The airfield was first used in World War I as a bombing and ground-attack range for aircraft flying from elsewhere in the area. The base was abandoned in 1918 but was resurrected in 1940 to serve as a decoy airfield to RAF Mildenhall just five miles away, being equipped with false lights, runways and dummy aircraft.

From late 1941 Lakenheath became an overspill airfield for Mildenhall, with Short Stirling aircraft visiting, and eventually being based here full time from the 6th April 1942, the day the base became fully operational. At least half of the flying operations were involved with mine laying activities. These Short Stirlings moved out in 1944 to make way for Boeing B-29 Superfortresses of the United States Air Force. For this the runways needed to be upgraded and lengthened, a task that was not completed until after the end of the war. The base was downgraded to a 'care and maintenance' status only, but with the Cold War looming it was re-opened in May 1948. In July the first B-29 Superfortresses arrived for a temporary ninety day deployment. The Americans never left, and on the 27th November 1948 operational control was transferred to the United States Air Force.

For two days in 1997 R.A.F. Lakenheath doubled as an American airbase in the South China Sea for *Tomorrow Never Dies*. This is where James Bond meets Jack Wade and establishes that the G.P.S. encoder has been tampered with. A clue to the true location is that all the F-15s in shot bear LN markings, indicating that they are based at Lakenheath.

JAMES BOND IN SURREY
CRANLEIGH - DUNSFOLD AERODROME

[The prototype Skyfleet S570 airliner at Miami airport during the filming of *Casino Royale*]

Cranleigh, near Guildford, proclaims itself the largest village in England. It had its own railway station from 1865 with commuter services to Guildford and onward to London, but fell victim to the Beeching Axe in 1965. The parish church of Saint Nicholas dates from around 1170, the building in its present form being of mid-14th century origin but extensively restored in 1847. It is thought by some that the gargoyle, situated on a pillar inside the church, was the inspiration for the Cheshire Cat in *Alice in Wonderland* since Lewis Carroll lived locally in Guildford. One former local resident whose name will be familiar to most is Barbara Bach, who at one time lived on the outskirts of the village with her then husband, Ringo Star.

Approximately four miles to the west of the village is Dunsfold Aerodrome, now part of Dunsfold Park. The site was first occupied on the 11th May 1942 by the First Canadian Army, who after twenty weeks work had built an airfield that became operational on the 16th October 1942. From that point onwards a variety of aircraft, including B-25 Mitchell bombers, Typhoons, Mustangs, Mosquitoes and Spitfires, all used the base.

175

After the war nearly fifty thousand prisoners of war were repatriated here, mainly in Dakota, Lancaster, Stirling and Halifax aircraft, before the aerodrome was designated as inactive in August 1946. It became active again when Skyways Ltd. used the airfield during the Berlin Airlift in 1948-49. They went into liquidation in 1950, but the site was then leased to the Hawker Aircraft Company Ltd. who used the base as a centre for testing and refurbishing Sea Hawks, Hunters, Sea Furies, Gnats, Harriers and Hawks for worldwide markets. It also supported various British operations and services involvement abroad. It was here that in May 1953 Neville Duke set a new world air speed record at an average speed of 727.63 miles per hour in a prototype Hunter Mk 3. In October 1960 the forerunner of the Harrier Jump Jet made its first tethered flight at Dunsfold, which led to its first conventional flight the following month. In 2000 Hawker, by then part of BAe Systems, moved out, clearing the way for the creation of Dunsfold Park, which is designated as a private unlicensed airfield, but is now also the home to around a hundred local businesses.

The airfield will be familiar to many television viewers, since this is the home of the BBC *Top Gear* team. In addition there have been many other film appearances including, most notably, *Nanny McPhee Returns* (2010), *The Da Vinci Code* (2006), *Batman Begins* (2005) and *Johnny English Reborn* (2011), while on the small screen Dunsfold may be spotted in *Spooks*, *Day of the Triffids* and *Foyle's War*, which have all been shot on location here.

[The Skyfleet S570 model exhibiting double engines and extra fuel tanks on the wings]

The exciting chase around Miami airport in *Casino Royale* was filmed at Dunsfold Park. In this sequence, Bond kills Carlos and foils Le Chiffre's attempt to destroy the prototype Skyfleet S570 airliner in order to make a killing on the stock market. The aircraft seen on screen is a modified Boeing 747. Originally it had been intended to use an Airbus A380 but the aeroplane was not ready in time, so in the event an ex-British Airways, Air

Asia and Malaysia Airlines aircraft that had been retired from service was refitted with two mock-up double engines attached to each inner pylon, along with external fuel tanks on the outer pylons. What is seen on the screen are real aircraft along with some computer generated images and a 19.6 foot model.

[Even for the model version of the Skyfleet S570 attention to detail is very much in evidence]

Dunsfold also features in *Quantum of Solace*, although no filming took place there (the airport scenes all being shot at Farnborough – page 109).

Recordings of aircraft engines at Dunsfold were used in the dogfight sequence, in which Bond and Camilla are shot down, but escape death by skydiving out of their burning aeroplane into a sinkhole.

ELSTEAD - HANKLEY COMMON

['Welcome to Scotland'. It is easy to see why Hankley Common could easily be mistaken for the Highlands. Here Skyfall is being erected prior to filming along with the chapel to the left of the picture]

Hankley and Elstead Commons lie within the Longmoor Training Area of the Ministry of Defence. They represent some of the finest remaining heathland in Southern England and are nationally important for their bird, reptile and invertebrate populations. The area is covered with both common and bell heather, along with bracken and woodlands of birch and Scots Pine.

Hankley Common is designated a Site of Special Scientific Interest, an in addition in 1996 the whole area was given a Forest of Excellence award by the Forestry Commission, reflecting the exceptional management of the landscape, wildlife conservation, timber production and public access in the area. Army training is limited to logistics and minor infantry manoeuvre exercises. The public are permitted along public rights of way at all times.

In 1943, in an area of the common called Lion's Mouth, Canadian troops built a replica section of the Atlantic Wall, the fortifications erected by the Germans along the western coast of Europe. The replica was used in training Allied troops for the D-Day landings in Normandy. It is around one hundred metres long and was divided into two sections, between which were huge steel gates. There were other obstacles nearby, such as huge concrete blocks, lengths of railway track set in concrete, and wire entanglements. Today two huge breaches in the main wall are the most obvious scars left by the live weapons training, but there are many more. A year earlier Hankley Common was the scene of the 'Wigwam Girl' murder. A girl named Joan Wolfe, who had been living in a crude shelter resembling a wigwam, was stabbed to death shortly after informing a Canadian soldier August Sangret, that she was pregnant by him. Circumstantial evidence all pointed to Sangret and he was hanged for her murder at Wandsworth Prison on the 29th April 1943.

[Skyfall under construction in early 2012]

Hankley Common has featured in the *Doctor Who* serial *The Silurians*, *Tenko* and the comedy *Blackadder: Back and Forth*. In *Ultimate Force* it became a training camp for some Colombian soldiers. James Bond has visited here twice, first in *The World Is Not Enough*, when he and Doctor Christmas are nearly killed while trying to diffuse the bomb on the inspection rig in the King oil pipeline. The exterior shots of the pipeline were filmed in Wales (page 225) while the actual explosion of the pipeline section was performed at Hankley Common. By far the most memorable use of the common to date was in *Skyfall*, when it doubled perfectly as

Scotland. The childhood home of Bond, Skyfall, was built as a full scale model using plywood and plaster (along with a chapel nearby). Initially Duntrune Castle in Scotland was also to feature, with part of a boat chase being filmed but never completed. Skyfall was supposed to be based on the Scottish estate of Robert Fleming, the international financier and grandfather of Ian Fleming.

[The British Army on exercise arriving a little late at the spot where Skyfall once stood. The track leading down from the ridge is where the entrance to Skyfall was located, and from where the 'men coming to kill us' emerge at the end of the film]

Bond and M are met at Skyfall by Kincade, the gamekeeper, and between them they improvise a series of traps throughout the house to enable them to repel Silva's men. Silva subsequently arrives by helicopter with a second wave of men, and after the climatic fight sequence the resulting explosions cause the helicopter to crash, destroying the house and killing most of Silva's men. Silva escapes and follows Kincade and M to the chapel where both are to die despite Bond's best efforts to save his boss.

EPSOM - EPSOM DOWNS RACECOURSE

[Not many would confuse this building with St. Petersburg airport. The Queen's Stand where filming took place for *GoldenEye* is to the left in the bottom picture]

Epsom lies in a valley of the Epsom Downs, just sixteen miles from Charing Cross: within the commuter belt but separate from London. The name derives from that of a Saxon landowner, Ebba, whose properties also included Effingham, Bookham and Cheam. At the time of the Domesday

Book, Epsom, recorded as Evesham and held by Chertsey Abbey, comprised thirty-eight peasant households, two churches and two mills. In the 17th century Epsom was well known as a spa, and magnesium sulphate, originally obtained by boiling down water from the town's bitter saline spring, is still commonly called Epsom salts.

However, the town is most famous for the adjacent Epsom Downs racecourse, where two of the five English Classic horse races are run: the Oaks and the Derby. The first recorded race here was in 1661. In 1779 Edward Smith-Stanley, 12th Earl of Derby, organised a race for three-year-old fillies, calling it the Oaks after his estate at Carshalton. It was so successful that the following year he introduced another race, this time for colts and fillies, which he named the Derby. Tragedy struck at the Derby on the 4th June 1913, when a suffragette, Emily Davison, threw herself in front of King George V's horse, bringing him down and fatally injuring herself.

In 1925 Stanley Wootton bought land on Walton Downs and leased land on Epsom Downs. His aim was to preserve training and racing at Epsom, while still allowing public access, and in fact the land is still open to the public at all times, subject only to certain by-laws. The opportunity to watch the racing free of charge has long meant that the Derby is the most attended sporting event in the country, though today it is almost impossible to get a good view without paying.

In *GoldenEye* the rear of the Queen's Stand represents St. Petersburg airport, where Bond meets Jack Wade as he exits the building. Interestingly, another racecourse, Ascot, was used most recently in *Skyfall* to double as Shanghai airport (page 21).

STANWELL - ESSO WEST LONDON TERMINAL

The village of Stanwell may have been named after St. Anne's well, or, more probably, its name just means 'stone well'. In 1603 Lord Knyvett, the man who arrested Guy Fawkes, was granted the manor of Stanwell. In 1838 an unknown species of rose was found in a local garden and became the Stanwell Perpetual. Stanwell is at the very north of the county and less than half a mile from the southern boundary of Heathrow airport, many of the residents being employees there.

In Belfont Road, which runs parallel to the Southern Perimeter Road of Heathrow, is the Esso West London Terminal, which is strategically located on 33 acres of land, close to both the airport and the M25. It serves a large tributary area stretching from Milton Keynes in the north, to Brighton on the south coast, from Swindon in the west to much of London to the east.

[The storage tanks at Stanwell are still instantly recognisable as those used in filming the pre-title sequence in *Goldfinger*]

The terminal, consisting of twenty-two cylindrical storage tanks, was built in 1964 but has been modernised and developed several times. The terminal is connected to the Fawley refinery, near Southampton, via a proprietary Esso pipeline.

In 2011 a new vapour recovery unit with a greater capacity was built, and all the tank bunds (a liquid collection facility which in the event of a leak or spillage from the tanks or pipes will capture well in excess of the liquids held within them) were upgraded. Seventeen of the terminal's tanks are in use and have between them an overall capacity of some 100,000 cubic metres. The products available are both diesel and petrol for motor vehicles, as well as aviation fuel. The site is open twenty-four hours a day and is only closed on Christmas Day itself.

When the opening shots of *Goldfinger* were filmed here in early 1964 the site was still under construction with the tanks all empty, and so there was no danger of explosion due to the presence of a film crew.

[Door to a villain's hideout?]

The scene is supposedly set in South America, where the villain has a drug factory inside one of the storage tanks. Bond gains entry via a revolving door disguised as an outlet and subsequently blows up the tank – all within the first two minutes of the film. Maybe the authorities should take a closer look at the West London Terminal in view of the fact that there are presently five unused tanks!

JAMES BOND IN WEST SUSSEX

AMBERLEY - AMBERLEY MUSEUM & HERITAGE CENTRE

[The Railway Exhibition Hall with no sign of Zorin's airship emerging over the chalk hill behind]

The little village of Amberley near Arundel, one of the prettiest on the South Downs, is notable for its many thatched cottages. Beside the 11th century church of St. Michael is Amberley Castle, originally a fortified manor house, later a fortress for the Bishops of Chichester, and now a well-regarded hotel. There are regular trains from Amberley station to London, Portsmouth and Bognor Regis.

Next to the station, in a former chalk quarry, is Amberley Museum and Heritage Centre, where several kilns and associated buildings are preserved on a 36 acre site, including offices, bagging shed and locomotive shed. Founded in 1979, the museum is dedicated to the industrial heritage of South East England, with a special interest in communications and transport. From the 1840s to the 1960s chalk was quarried from several pits – the three main ones being the White Pit, the Grey Pit and the South Pit – and burnt in the kilns to produce lime for mortar and for agricultural fertiliser. A century ago this was the largest works of its kind in the region.

The two largest of the preserved kilns are situated in the quarry bottom beyond the timber yard. Built in around 1905 to the design of a Belgian engineer named De Witt, they comprised eighteen firing chambers operated on a down-draught principle, but they were not a success, probably owing to the poor circulation of gases through the chambers. In 1910 a series of conventional inverted-bottle-shaped chambers was let in to the structure. It was inside one of the De Witt kilns that May Day escaped drowning in *A View to a Kill*, by climbing up what was supposed to be a mineshaft.

There is much more to be seen on the museum's large site, including the Southdown Bus garage, a reconstructed 1920s depot housing working buses; the Village Garage, a reconstructed 1930s motor repair shop; Paviors Hall of Road Making, located in a 19th century iron-framed industrial building and telling the story of road construction from the earliest times; the fire station, a reconstruction of a 1950s building, containing historic fire engines and other equipment; the late 19th century brickyard drying shed, housing an exhibition on the local brickmaking industry; the EDF Energy Electricity Hall, displaying a wide range of electrical equipment from small domestic appliances to heavy engineering plant for the mains supply system; the Hall of Tools, an exhibition with associated demonstrations by the Tools and Trades History Society; the Vintage Wireless and Communications exhibition, which features all manner of telegraph, radio and telephone equipment, including some clandestine sets from World War II; and the BT Connected Earth telecommunications exhibition, part of a project founded to safeguard BT's unique heritage of telecommunications artefacts, dating back to the earliest days of telegraphy.

[Thakenham skips painted in Zorin livery were used in filming (left), one being preserved in the Railway Exhibition Hall (right)]

For the James Bond enthusiast, however, the main attraction is the Amberley Museum Railway, a narrow gauge railway and exhibition hall, devoted to British industrial narrow gauge railways. (In its working days the quarry had its own standard gauge railway, connected to the main line.)

Among the current rolling stock are several skip wagons bearing the 'Zorin Green' livery.

[Entrance to the Main Strike Mine as it was in 1984 during filming (left) and as it is today (right)]

The whole site was closed for three weeks during 1984 while the place was transformed into the Main Strike Mine, supposedly in Silicon Valley, California. The preparation for this key sequence in *A View to a Kill* took two weeks with up to two hundred production staff on site at any one time. All the internal filming for the mine was done back at Pinewood Studios (page 45) but using railway track, locomotives (the two standard Hudson-Hunslet diesels) and some Thakenham skips, all on loan from Amberley.

In the film it will be recalled that, just after May Day's climb up the flooded mineshaft, she rather heroically sacrifices herself and is blown up by Zorin's bomb as she emerges from the mine entrance while holding off the brake on one of the railway trucks. This was shot on the old south curve of the railway triangle, which has since been reconfigured, although even today it is easy to recognise the location.

The very next scene involved Stacey Sutton running down from the surrounding hill towards Bond, but unfortunately she does not see, or hear, Zorin's airship just behind her. Zorin leans out and grabs her and as the airship gains height, Bond, in hot pursuit, clings onto the trailing guideline.

He is seen leaving Amberley hanging precariously underneath the airship, and moments later is over San Francisco and heading for the film's climax at the Golden Gate Bridge.

[Looking out from the Main Strike Mine entrance to where May Day was killed (top). He's behind you! Photograph taken during the filming at Amberley in 1984]

[Roger Moore having a well deserved break, and looking pretty relaxed considering that he is about to dangle below an airship for several thousand miles]

Amberley Museum & Heritage Centre makes a great day out for all the family. It is open Wednesday-Sunday from around March to November, as well as every day during the Spring half-term school holiday, Bank Holiday Mondays throughout the season and for special Christmas events. The adult admission price is around £10 with various discounts available for families, students etc. For full details please visit www.amberleymuseum.co.uk.

FOR BOND LOVERS ONLY!
www.007magazine.com
Publishing the best of Bond internationally since 1979

JAMES BOND IN WILTSHIRE

SWINDON - SPECTRUM BUILDING
VYGON (EX MOTOROLA) BUILDING

[The Spectrum Building, known by locals as the old Renault Building, was opened in 1983 and made an appearance in *A View to a Kill*]

Swindon, midway between Bristol and Reading, was originally a Saxon settlement, and later a small market town until the mid-19th century. Its growth started in 1810 with the construction of the Wilts and Berks Canal, followed swiftly by the North Wilts Canal in 1819. However, this was nothing compared to what commenced in 1841 when Isambard Kingdom Brunel chose Swindon, because of its central location on his London to Bristol railway, as the centre for repair and maintenance of locomotives on the Great Western Railway. At its peak the workshops employed over fourteen thousand people. In 1960 the last British steam locomotive, *Evening Star*, was built here, but by the 1970s much of the works had closed, and full closure came in 1986. However, this was not the end of heavy engineering in Swindon for it has managed to attract new companies to the area, including Honda, who converted an old Vickers factory at the former RAF South Marston into a car plant. Other companies such as Motorola, Dolby Labs, Intel, Vygon (UK) Limited and the National Trust are all large local employers, and just as well since the current population is close to two hundred thousand.

Perhaps Swindon's most acclaimed piece of architecture is Sir Norman Foster's former Renault Distribution Centre, officially called the Spectrum

Building. It was designed according to the company's belief that 'to become recognisable within your market, you must become recognisable in the environment', and with its unique structure featuring a large yellow roof, the building needed no sign to identify the company: the roof was enough. It was opened, on the 15th June 1983, by the French Secretary of State for Consumer Affairs, Madame Catherine Lalumiere. The structure, which is Grade II listed and won the *Financial Times* award for Architecture at Work in 1984, is made up of forty-two identical twenty-four metre square bays, which acted as a warehouse, distribution centre, offices, showroom, training school and site restaurant. Renault moved out in 2001, and after being empty for several years it is now home to several organisations, including a play centre for children. In 1984 filming took place here for a small scene in *A View to a Kill* with both Roger Moore and Patrick Magnee in attendance. In the film the building, although it is only the inside that is seen, is meant to be part of the Chantilly estate of Max Zorin in France. At night Bond and Tibbett break into Zorin's laboratory below the stables and discover that he is implanting adrenaline-releasing devises in his horses in order to improve performance. However, an alarm is set off, and the two escape via Zorin's automated warehouse, where several henchmen are dispatched in the tongue in cheek manner that had become the trademark of the Roger Moore films. It was these warehouse scenes that were shot in the Renault building.

[Even with the cut down services tube the old Motorola Building is impressive, albeit not very Turkish in appearance]

Another iconic structure in Swindon is the Motorola Building at Groundwell, currently the distribution centre for drug company Vygon (UK) Limited. The futuristic structure was opened by Her Majesty the

Queen in 1998 and was designed to be the major manufacturing facility for Motorola's GSM radio transmission equipment. It took a year to build at a cost of £40 million. The construction is of aluminium and glass, the main complex covering an area equivalent to three football pitches end-to-end, and large enough to accommodate one thousand three hundred staff. The most prominent feature is the high-tech exposed steelwork and roof-level services tube, which being over five metres in diameter is large enough to drive a car through. The building won an award for architect Sheperd Robson in the 1999 Structural Steel Design Awards, and was also highly commended at the British Construction Industry Awards. Unfortunately the manufacture of mobile telephones ceased in 2001, although Motorola continued their presence here as it became their European headquarters for Home & Network Mobility, and in 2009 they built the first test-bed for the 4G broadband system on site. However, later that year the building was sold to Vygon (UK) Limited, who currently use the site as a distribution centre, with the consequence that the services tube being surplus to requirements was partially demolished. Two days filming took place here with all the main stars being present for *The World Is Not Enough* in 1999. The building serves as Electra King's Turkish headquarters at which M arrives by helicopter.

MISCELLANEOUS LOCATIONS

HIGHWORTH - THE GOLDFINGER TAVERN

[Despite the exterior this 'James Bond' location is well worth a visit]

Located just 6 miles to the north-east of Swindon, Highworth is noted for its Queen Anne style architecture and Georgian buildings. Until the mid-19th century this market town with a current population of around twelve thousand people was larger than Swindon.

However, it is to a rather more modern 1970s building in Newburgh Place that the James Bond enthusiast should make tracks, for here will be found the only public house in the country named after an Ian Fleming book, The Goldfinger Tavern. Perhaps not the place for a Martini (shaken but not stirred) it is nevertheless a fine local public house with a warm welcome, serving the community with drinks, food and regular entertainment nights.

SEVENHAMPTON - SEVENHAMPTON PLACE
ST. JAMES' CHURCH

At the bottom of a valley, a little closer to Swindon, is Sevenhampton. The earliest records for the village are from 1212, when it appears as Suvenhantone, which in Old English roughly translates as the town of the dwellers at the seven wells. Locally the place is known for Roves Farm Visitor Centre, a family run farm park with lots of hands-on farmyard attractions, including tractor rides and animal handling.

[Entrance to the Fleming estate in Sevenhampton]

In 1959 Ian Fleming and his wife Ann bought Warneford Place, a large 16th century house at the edge of the village. They had the old house pulled down and a modern dwelling erected in its place, a process that took four years. The Flemings had hardly moved into their new home when, in 1964, Ian was struck down by his second, and fatal, heart attack at the age of just fifty-six. Any potential visitors should note that the house is not visible from the road, and is closed to the public.

Almost next door to the Fleming estate is the church of St. James, where Fleming is buried under a simple obelisk, balanced on four spheres, tucked away in a corner of the graveyard and surrounded by twenty or more gravestones.

[The simple memorial to Ian, Ann and Caspar Fleming]

In October 1975, Fleming's son Caspar killed himself with an overdose of barbiturates and was buried alongside his father. He was twenty-three years old. Ann Fleming, who never really recovered from Ian's death, died in 1981 and was buried with her husband and their son.

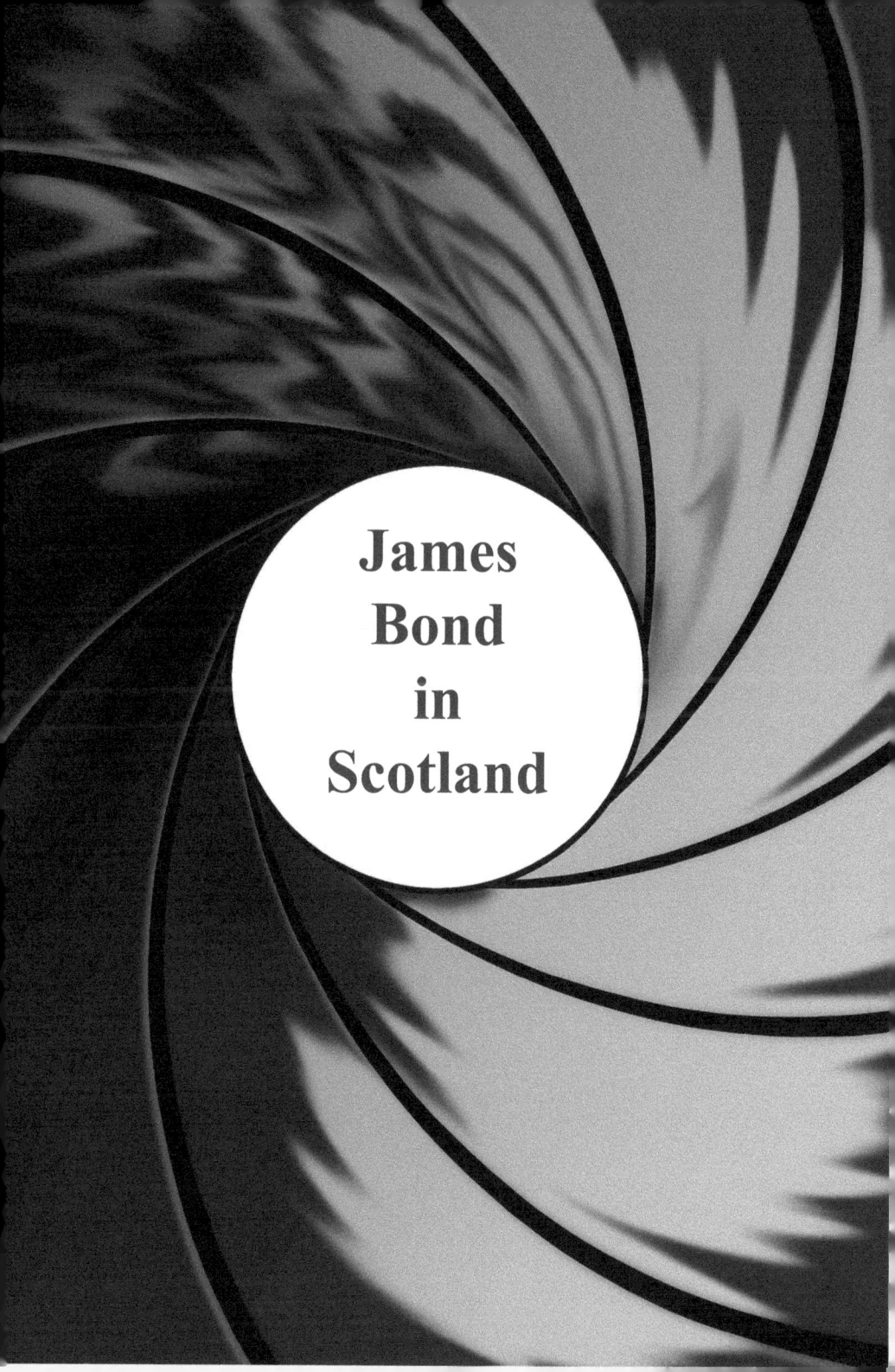

James Bond in Scotland

JAMES BOND IN ARGYLL AND BUTE

GARELOCHHEAD - H.M. NAVAL BASE CLYDE

[In *The Spy Who Loved Me* Bond's helicopter lands in the vicinity of the two cranes at the centre of the picture, and next to the large submarine dry dock building to the right, the inside of which could be mistaken for that in Stromberg's supertanker, Liparus]

The unitary authority of Argyll and Bute, to the north-west of Glasgow, was carved out of the former Strathclyde Region in 1996. It covers most of the county of Argyll and parts of the counties of Bute and Dunbartonshire. The southern islands of the Inner Hebrides, including Islay, Colonsay, Jura, Iona, Mull, Staffa and Tiree, fall within the council area, as of course does the Isle of Bute. The administrative centre is Lochgilphead.

Garelochhead on Loch Gare is the closest village to H.M. Naval Base Clyde, whose main site at Faslane is the home of the United Kingdom Submarine Service and the country's strategic nuclear deterrent, in the form of nuclear submarines armed with Trident missiles.

Long before the existence of the naval base the area was well known, due the advent of steamer cruising in the 1820s, and the opening of the West Highland Railway in 1894, as a popular tourist destination for those living in Glasgow just 25 miles away. This prompted an expansion of the village with some fine large houses being built for the prosperous classes. Several of these, such as Belmore House and the Shandon Hydropathic Institute, are today located within the naval base perimeter. However, by the late 20th century tourism had declined, and the naval base and the deepwater oil tanker terminal at Finnart on Loch Long provided the only major employment in the area.

Presently there are around four thousand civilian workers, and three thousand service personnel stationed at Faslane. The Clyde Naval Base's other site is the armaments depot at Coulport beside Loch Long, some 8 miles away. The shore establishment at Faslane is designated H.M.S. Neptune. Both Loch Gare and Loch Long are sea lochs extending to the Firth of Clyde, making Faslane an ideal location since not only is it secluded and deep, but easy to navigate with ready access to the North Atlantic.

[H.M.S. Astute, one of the latest generation hunter-killer nuclear submarines, approaching its home base at Faslane]

Faslane itself was a base as far back as World War II, when the whole bay was turned into a huge marshalling yard to serve this military port. Later it became a ship-breaking yard, dismantling amongst others the battleship H.M.S. Vanguard. In 1968 it became the home for the Polaris nuclear missile system, which was eventually installed on four submarines (H.M.S. Resolution, Repulse, Renown and Revenge respectively). At the time of *The Spy Who Loved Me* in 1977 the Polaris nuclear deterrent on H.M.S. Ranger (in the film), and the possible tracking of it from its wake would have seemed highly topical.

As well as the nuclear fleet, the base is also home to some conventional vessels, and indeed it is a conventional submarine that is seen in the background as Bond, following his meeting at the base, walks along the quay talking with Sir Frederick Gray from the Ministry of Defence.

KILMICHAEL GLASSARY - BARRACHUILE

[General view showing the area used to film the truck chase in *From Russia With Love*]

In *From Russia With Love* the two key chase sequences in which Bond, Romanova and the Lector decoding machine are pursued by SPECTRE, first by helicopter and then by boat, were both filmed in Scotland.

It will be recalled that once they have left the Orient Express, following the dispatch of Grant, they hijack his getaway truck (and driver) and proceed cross country heading for Venice. The actual location for filming this sequence was close to Kilmichael Glassary, a small settlement lying between Lorn and Knapdale on the west bank of the River Add and 4 miles from Lochgilphead. It was an early Christian centre associated with nearby Dunadd, and the location of a cattle market. It is best known for the prehistoric cup and ring carvings found on a natural rock outcrop along the Kilmartin Glen road. If you travel further up the glen you will cross the river twice, passing some standing stones on the left, before reaching an old sawmill where you should turn right. From here the road becomes a dirt track and only suitable for 4x4 vehicles. It was on this road between Barrachuile and Knockalava (to the left) that Bond was found running across the moor, jumping over rocks and eventually shooting down a helicopter. It is hard to identify the locations used, but even today there is evidence, if you know where to look, of the burnt-out SPECTRE helicopter. Please note, though, that this is strictly private land and you will not be welcomed if you trespass.

[The road along which the truck first appears (top), where Bond is seen running pursued by the helicopter (middle) and the actual rock Bond jumps over just prior to shooting down the helicopter (bottom)]

[Now more overgrown than when filming took place in 1963, this is the spot where the SPECTRE helicopter crashes]

The sequence in which Bond runs across the moor, stumbling and falling as the helicopter flies low over him, was deliberately shot in a similar style to the scene in classic Alfred Hitchcock film *North By Northwest* (1959), in which Cary Grant evades a crop sprayer. Most of the stunt work was performed by Sean Connery himself.

It will come as no surprise to learn that a radio-controlled model was destroyed in the filming, rather than a real helicopter. It was about six feet long and powered by a small petrol engine. When the helicopter explodes that there appears to be a wire holding it up, so it might be assumed that the helicopter was simply on a gantry and lowered. This would be erroneous, since the helicopter flew perfectly well in its own right, although it did have modified rotors to hold it in a stable condition for filming. The wire in shot is in fact a power cable used to set the explosives off in the main and tail rotors, since at that time radio control was not as sophisticated as today and could not be relied on. In fact this was the first time such a stunt had been tried on film.

Finally the quip made by Bond that "I'd say one of their aircraft was missing" was an in-joke not in the original script. The line was suggested by the production designer, Syd Caine, whose very first film had been *One of Our Aircraft Is Missing* (1942).

LOCH CRAIGNISH - LUNGA PIER
CRINAN
CRAOBH HAVEN

[Looking across Loch Craignish towards Loch Crinan close to where the SPECTRE boats start firing at Bond]

Loch Craignish is a sea loch about 6 miles long between Oban and the Crinan Canal. It opens into the Sound of Jura and provides a safe anchorage for small craft. In prehistoric times it was a crossroads for settlers between Ireland and the Great Glen. There are several small islands in the loch, the largest being Eilean Righ, Eilean Mhic Chrion and Island Macaskin. In *From Russia With Love* the SPECTRE boat chase was filmed along this stretch of coastline over a period of some weeks, the segment where Bond is under fire from grenade launchers and machine guns taking place at the seaward end of Loch Craignish itself.

The sequence starts with Bond and Romanova arriving in their truck, now showing no sign of smoke damage from its encounter with the SPECTRE helicopter (see page 203), at Lunga Pier, where there is a Fairey Huntress 23 speedboat complete with a custom fuel drum rack waiting for them. In the film this is supposed to be somewhere along the Dalmatian Coast, and indeed it was originally intended to film in Turkey near Istanbul, but the production crew were hampered by bad weather and choppy seas, which meant that the boats could not go at full speed, resulting in the shot footage looking too tame for a Bond film. Worse still, one of the camera boats on hire sank, so it was decided to relocate to Scotland where surely they would have better luck. They did not. Originally ten days were allocated for the boat chase sequence, but bad weather (this time due to the wind being in the wrong direction for the explosive finale) added another five days –

mainly because of Cubby Broccoli's perfectionism, insisting that they wait to get the shot just right. Worst of all, on Sunday 6th July, when the director, Terence Young, and art director, Michael White, set off by helicopter to scout for locations, the chopper developed engine trouble, flipped on to its side, plunged fifty feet into the water and promptly sank. Luckily there were no serious injuries. The crew managed to break the Plexiglas canopy and escape to the surface. Terence Young, according to reports, was back on set within the hour and shooting as if nothing had happened.

[Lunga Pier is little changed since 1963]

Much of the area lies within the Lunga Estates, which comprise Lunga House hotel and six cottages and cabins for rent, all set in four thousand acres of woodland on the Craignish peninsula. It is said to be one of the most beautiful and, though only 22 miles south of Oban, least-known parts of Scotland. Other attractions include Lunga Riding Stables, and the Forestry Commission's woodland walks in an area where beavers have been re-introduced.

[As Bond's boat sets out from Lunga Pier this is the panorama
seen in the background (top) while much of the subsequent
filming took place near Loch Crinan, the main actors
and film crew stayed at the Crinan Hotel (bottom)]

Once the boat is under way Bond's next task is to dispose of excess baggage by pushing the truck driver overboard, with the quip, "Just isn't your day, is it?" Most of the following shots of the boat were taken on Loch Crinan, just around the headland. The principal actors and crew stayed at the famous Crinan Hotel, where they were reportedly treated like royalty. The hotel is renowned for its fine seafood restaurant and its art gallery (www.crinanhotel.com). Right next to the hotel is the lock that gives entry to the Crinan Canal, which provides a direct link between the Clyde Estuary and the Inner Hebrides without the need to go around the long Kintyre peninsula. Along the fifteen-mile long canal are, appropriately, fifteen locks.

[Bond's Fairey Huntress 23 as seen in *From Russia With Love*]

On the other side of the hotel is the boatyard where Bond's Fairey Huntress 23 speedboat (the 23 indicates the vessel's length in feet) was berthed during filming, along with the two Huntresses and two Huntsman 28s used by the villains. One of the boats was driven by the test pilot Peter Twiss, the first man to fly at over 1,000 mph, who rehearsed for the chase in front of the hotel, including practising the deployment of the petrol drums in the water.

Even now there were problems with filming since, although the boats were very fast, their engines were so refined that even at full speed they only produced a whining noise described as being akin to that of a vacuum cleaner. What the audience would expect to hear was a roar of engines to accompany such a dramatic sequence. Luckily the sound engineer had in addition recorded the boats starting up in the harbour, and this sound is dubbed over the original soundtrack for the entire three-and-a-half minute chase sequence.

[Looking out from the causeway to the islands between which Bond ignites the fuel drums in *From Russia With Love*]

At the climax to the chase Bond deploys the petrol drums, which have been shot full of holes by the pursuing SPECTRE boats, and then appears to surrender. In fact this is a trap, as Bond now fires his Verey pistol into the disengaged fuel drums causing an inferno, which incinerates Morzeny and the rest of the villains, allowing Bond and Romanova to continue to Venice. From the moment that the boats ignite it is not Scotland that we see but the Paddock Tank at Pinewood (page 45), but even now, despite the controlled conditions, there was a serious incident. Three stuntmen were injured and Walter Gotell, playing the villain Morzeny, had his eyelids burnt. The explosions were so loud it was reported that crockery in the Pinewood commissary rattled.

The location used was what is now Craobh Haven (not to be confused with Crab Key in *Dr. No*) on the Craignish peninsula, close to Lunga Pier. At the time of filming this was merely an isolated stretch of water with several little islands between which hundreds of charges were set to create the effect of the exploding petrol drums. Even now things did not go right for the production crew, since due to a miscommunication the charges were set off during a rehearsal when the cameras were not running. John Stears, known as the 'Dean of Special Effects', had just one day to re-rig the hundreds of charges etc., which had to be brought overnight from London.

Finally, on Wednesday 17th July 1963, with a 6.00 am unit call, the scene was due to be completed, but again the film seemed jinxed. The driver bringing Daniela Bianchi, who played Tatiana Romanova, to the location fell asleep and crashed the car. The actress's face was bruised and her scenes had to be delayed for two weeks while the contusions healed.

Craobh Haven, located in the Firth of Lorne, and looking out towards the Slate islands, was built in 1983 as a holiday resort and marina. It was constructed by building large causeways and a breakwater between the group of small tidal saltwater islands. The village has a public house, The Lord of the Isles, run by the Lunga Estates, a store, harbourmaster and marine office, and a water sports centre as well as holiday accommodation on the island of Eilean Buidhe. The marina is completely sheltered and popular with private boat owners, and although there are no facilities for larger vessels some small cruise ships do anchor off the marina and ferry their passengers ashore for onward sightseeing trips. The marina is also a base for diving expeditions to the nearby Garvellachs. The waters here are somewhat devoid of fish but are very clear and have an extensive array of corals, starfish, anemones and various shellfish, as well as porpoises and the occasional Minke whale, while in the air Golden Eagles and Sea Eagles are common.

The waters may seem tranquil but weather conditions can change here very quickly. In addition there are some treacherous stretches of water, due to the array of separate tidal races produced by the underwater topography. Between the islands of Lunga and Scarba is the fearsome Grey Dogs tidal race, and to the south of Scarba, in the Gulf of Corryvreckan, is the notorious Corryvreckan whirlpool, the third largest in the world. It surrounds an underwater pyramid of basalt, which rises from a depth of seventy metres below the surface to twenty-nine metres at its peak. The currents can reach over ten knots and produce waves more than nine metres high, and at times, it is said, the roar can be heard ten miles away.

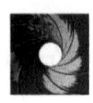

MISCELLANEOUS LOCATION
DUNTRUNE - DUNTRUNE CASTLE

[Duntrune Castle stands imposingly as if guarding Loch Crinan]

On the north side of Loch Crinan, directly opposite the Crinan Hotel, is Duntrune Castle, reputedly the oldest continuously occupied castle on the Scottish mainland. One of several strongholds built by the MacDougall clan in the 12th century, Duntrune Castle was later acquired by the Campbells, who in 1644 had to defend it against their bitter rivals the MacDonalds, commanded by Alasdair Mac Colla. The Campbells sold Duntrune in 1792, to the Malcolms of Poltalloch, and the present owner is Robin Neill Malcolm, current chief of the Clan Malcolm. The castle is a category B listed building.

All good castles have a ghost, and Duntrune is no exception: it is said to be haunted by a handless piper. Two legends are told of how he came to be there. The certain fact is that during renovations at the castle a man's skeleton was found beneath a stone path, the hands cleanly severed at the wrists.

According to one story, Mac Colla had sent the piper to the castle as a spy. He was quickly discovered by the Campbells and imprisoned, but he played his pipes to warn the MacDonalds that their impending attack was expected. They retreated, but in retaliation the Campbells cut off the piper's hands. The alternative tale is that the MacDonalds took the castle, but Mac Colla needed to return home, leaving only a small force behind, including his personal piper. The Campbells recaptured the castle and slew the defenders, all except the piper. Then they waited patiently for the MacDonalds to return. When Mac Colla's boat was sighted, the piper was ordered to play a tune of welcome, but he actually sounded a warning, and the MacDonalds turned back. As punishment for foiling their trap, the piper's hands were cut off, and he bled to death. (A more cynical suggestion is that the mutilation was a blow struck on behalf of music lovers throughout the world!)

[Might this have been the original entrance to Skyfall?]

Duntrune Castle could have been Skyfall. The original intention was to shoot the film's climax here, and the entire cast and crew were booked in at the castle, the Crinan Hotel and most of the other accommodation in the area. The decision to cancel caused considerable resentment among the locals, who dubbed the film *Dr. No Show*.

JAMES BOND IN HIGHLAND
DORNIE - EILEAN DONAN CASTLE

[Perhaps the most photographed and recognisable castle in the world, Eilean Donan Castle, as seen in *The World Is Not Enough*, is not a natural choice for a secret MI6 base in Scotland]

The Highland region, roughly speaking, is that mountainous and rugged part of Scotland to the north and west of the Highland Boundary Fault, which separates it from the Lowlands. The area is itself divided by the Great Glen into the Grampian Mountains (to the southeast) and the Northwest Highlands. The highest mountain in the British Isles, Ben Nevis, is here. Before the 19th century the population was much larger, but a combination of factors, notably the reprisals that followed the Jacobite Rising of 1745, the infamous Highland Clearances, and mass migration to urban areas during the Industrial Revolution, led to a steep decline. The average population density in the Highlands and Islands is now said to be lower than that of Sweden, Norway, Papua New Guinea and Argentina.

Dornie is a small former fishing village near the meeting point of Loch Duich, Loch Aish and Loch Long. The main A87 road to Skye passes just outside the village, and today there is a bridge over Loch Long where until recent times there was a short ferry crossing. Adjacent to the bridge is Eilean Donan Castle, one of the most romantic and picturesque in the world, although its appearance today is mainly the result of rebuilding by Lt. Col. John MacRae-Gilstrap between 1912 and 1932.

The name is most likely derived from the 6th century Irish saint, Bishop Donan, who came to Scotland in around 580. It is also thought that the castle itself was originally constructed in the 13th century as a defence against Viking attacks. The castle fortifications evolved in stages over the years but by the early 18th century had largely fallen into disrepair, although it did play a small role in the third of the famous Jacobite Risings.

In April 1719 a party of Spanish soldiers occupied the castle, ready to support an expected Highland uprising – which never took place. On the 10th May HMS Worcester, HMS Flamborough, and HMS Enterprise anchored in the loch and sent a boat ashore under a flag of truce. However the Spanish soldiers fired at the boat, which was recalled, and all three ships opened fire on the castle for an hour or more. On the evening of the next day the ships' boats went ashore and captured the castle against little resistance. Inside were 'an Irishman, a captain, a Spanish lieutenant, a serjeant, one Scotch rebel and 39 Spanish soldiers, 343 barrels of powder and 52 barrels of musquet shot'. Demolition of the castle took two days and twenty-seven barrels of gunpowder. The castle then remained in ruins for best part of two hundred years, until John MacRae-Gilstrap, assisted by Farquhar MacRae, decided to restore it. Since 1983 the castle has been part of the Conchra Charitable Trust, established by the MacRae family to maintain and restore the property for future generations. If visiting please see www.eileandonancastle.com for more information.

Understandably it has featured in many films, as well as in advertising and packaging for typically Scottish products such as whisky. To date Eilean Donan can be spotted in no fewer than nineteen productions, most notably *Bonnie Prince Charlie* (1948), *The Master of Ballantrae* (1953), *Highlander* (1986), *Rob Roy* (1995), *Loch Ness* (1996), *Elizabeth: The Golden Age* (2007) and *Made of Honor* (2008). On the small screen, among many appearances, it featured in *The New Avengers* episode *The Eagle's Nest* as the place where Hitler's body, which had been cryogenically frozen, is being hidden by a group of monks.

All the interior scenes in *The World Is Not Enough* were filmed in the studio, but there is a brief establishing shot of Eilean Donan, with the statement that it is the Scottish HQ of MI6. A longer scene featuring Bond's Aston Martin was abandoned. In the visitor centre next to the ticket office is displayed one of the 'Bond 50' plaques given to prominent filming locations.

GLENCOE - GLEN ETIVE

[Looking down Glen Coe from the eastern end]

The area around Glen Coe (said to mean 'Glen of Weeping' although it is in fact named after the River Coe, which runs through it) is reckoned to be one of the most spectacular and beautiful places in Scotland. It is part of the designated National Scenic Area of Ben Nevis and Glen Coe, The narrow glen, which exhibits a grim grandeur, is of course best known for the infamous Massacre of Glencoe, which took place here in 1692.

In 1691, King William III, aware of rising Jacobite sympathisers, decreed that all clan chiefs should sign an oath of allegiance to him. However, MacIain of Glencoe (the MacIains are a sept of the Clan MacDonald) did not sign by the deadline of the 1st January 1692, despite arriving in Fort William to declare himself on New Year's Eve 1691. It transpired that he should have gone to Inveraray to swear his allegiance, which took until the 6th January. Thinking that this matter was now closed, he returned to the peace of Glencoe, but the King had other ideas.

Robert Campbell of Glenlyon, who was related by marriage to Maclain, along with one hundred and twenty-eight soldiers, went to Glencoe to collect the Cess tax. They were billeted with the MacDonalds for twelve days, and by all accounts were welcomed in a most hospitable manner. On the morning of 13th February 1692, following orders received the previous night from the newly arrived Captain Drummond, the soldiers turned on their hosts, killing thirty-eight of them, many while trying to escape into the snow-covered hills, while another forty women and children died of ensuing exposure after their homes were burnt. Maclain, who had been the reason for the massacre, died while trying to rise from his bed.

Afterwards there was an inquiry, since this was a clear example of what is termed 'Murder under Trust', but due to the fact that the King himself had countersigned the orders much was covered up, to the extent that, although a recommendation was made to punish the perpetrators (and to financially recompense the MacDonalds), while exonerating the King, nothing was actually done save for arresting John Campbell of Breadalbane. He remained in Edinburgh Castle for a few days on a different matter of high treason, having been involved in secret talks with Jacobite chiefs. Indeed the massacre became regarded not so much a government action, but as a consequence of clan rivalry between the MacDonalds and Campbells.

Turning to geology, the glen is a classic U-shape, formed by an Ice Age glacier, the floor of the glen being less than half a mile wide, narrowing sharply at the Pass of Glen Coe about half way along. Rannoch Moor is situated to the east (and this is the straight road that Bond and M are initially seen driving along in *Skyfall*), while Glen Etive runs to the south. In all, the road running through Glen Coe from the village of Glencoe in the west towards Rannoch Moor is around seven miles long.

Glen Coe was originally part of the lands of Clan Donald but is today owned by the National Trust for Scotland. The land was purchased by mountaineer and philanthropist Percy Unna, who then gave it to the trust on condition that it maintained the wild nature of the land. The building of a visitor centre caused some controversy, as some felt this to be a contravention of the gift. So the original centre was closed, and a new one built further down the glen nearer Glencoe village.

The population of Glen Coe is sparse, although there are signs of a flint factory dating to the Neolithic Age in North Ballachulish, and in the 1890s a wooden figure, named the Ballachulish Goddess, was found in the same area and subsequently dated to 626 BC. There is also evidence of an Iron Age fort in the vicinity, while at Achara there is a standing stone. Finally, it is even thought that the Vikings may have visited the area.

There is car parking at the scenic waterfalls in the Pass of Glen Coe, which was used as the location for the Bridge of Death and Gorge of Eternal Peril in the film *Monty Python and the Holy Grail* (1975). Other films to be made in this area include *The 39 Steps* (1935), *Bonnie Prince Charlie* (1948), *Kidnapped* (1960), *633 Squadron* (1964), *Highlander* (1986), *Being Human* (1993), *Braveheart* (1995), *Rob Roy* (1995), *Made of Honor* (2008) and of course the Harry Potter series, to a greater or lesser extent. Indeed, it is Glen Coe that provides much of the backdrop footage, and a film set comprising Hagrid's hut, the Bridge to Nowhere, four sets of standing stones, and a small chapel-like building was constructed here for *Harry Potter and the Prisoner of Azkaban* (2004) at a cost of £2 million.

[The spot on the Glen Etive road, close to Skyfall, where Bond takes a break from driving the Aston Martin and stands talking to M]

Further along Glen Coe on the right hand side, close to the Kings House Hotel, is a single track road with passing places, leading southwards along Glen Etive, and finishing at the top of Loch Etive some fourteen miles later. It is the original 'road to nowhere' but well worth the detour, since the scenery is superb. The road follows the path of the River Etive, which rises on the peaks surrounding Rannoch Moor, with several tributary systems coming together at the Kings Head Hotel. At the north end of the glen are two mountains known as the 'Shepherds of Etive' (*Buachaille Etive Mor* and *Buachaille Etive Beag*) while further down closer to the loch are Ben Starav and Beinn Fhionnlaidh. All four rise to around a thousand metres above sea level.

In *Skyfall* Bond and M are driving along this road when, just before Dalness, he stops the car for a reflective exchange about his childhood. For this scene two Aston Martin DB5s were used, one for driving shots and one for interior shots filmed on a low-loader. By chance there was a green DB5 at the Aston Martin Works about to undergo restoration, and so this car was chosen to be converted into a Bond car. Normally a full restoration would take upwards of fourteen months but EON gave a deadline of just seven weeks to have it ready in time for filming on 8th February 2012. In this time pressing structural work was carried out to make the vehicle road legal, the tan seats were re-coloured black, items such as the clock bezels were machined to be of Bond specification, carpets replaced and the bodywork repainted in Silver Birch with an outline painted to represent the ejector seat hatch in the roof. Just to ensure that the two cars to be used in filming were identical the EON DB5 from *GoldenEye* was trucked up to the Aston Martin Works in Newport Pagnell several times for comparison.

In all four cars were used to represent Bond's car. In the fight sequence at Skyfall the Aston Martin is destroyed by Silva's Merlin AW101 helicopter, but in fact no Aston Martins were harmed during filming. What we see on screen is a montage of a one-third scale model, prototyped in plastic, and the bodyshell of a Porsche 928 (which has a similar wheelbase and screen rakes to a DB5) fitted with genuine, but scrap, Aston Martin panels.

MISCELLANEOUS LOCATION
DALNESS - DALNESS LODGE

[Dalness Lodge with the peak of Stob na Broige behind]

Just a mile or so further along the Glen Etive road from the spot where Bond and M talk is Dalness Lodge. If anywhere, this is the real Skyfall, since it once belonged to the Fleming family. Although Ian Fleming never lived here, he certainly visited, and it is thought that this place was his inspiration to create a Scottish ancestry for James Bond in his penultimate novel, *You Only Live Twice*. In the book we are told that Bond's parents, Andrew and Monique Delacroix Bond, died in a climbing accident in the French Alps. In *Skyfall*, appropriately, Andrew and Monique's tombstone can be seen in the graveyard of the family chapel.

219

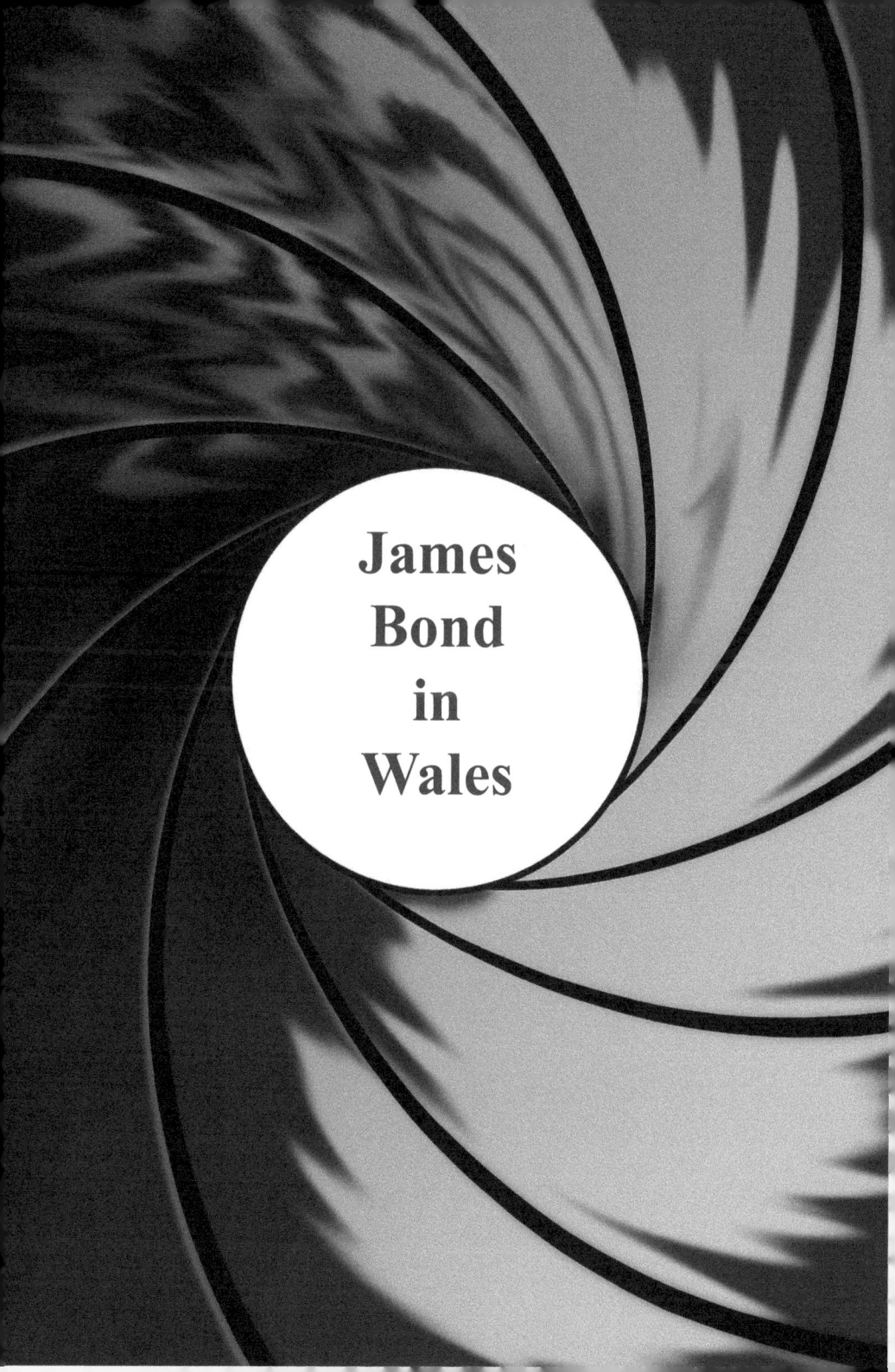

James Bond in Wales

JAMES BOND IN CARDIGANSHIRE
PENBRYN - PENBRYN BEACH

[Penbryn beach looking towards the headland used in *Die Another Die*]

The village of Penbryn is situated on the Ceredigion coast, about 10 miles up from Cardigan. The area consists largely of farms and caravan sites. Nearby is a monument dating from the early Christian period, known as the Corbalengi Stone, because of its inscription: 'CORBALENGI IACIT ORDOVS', which appears to mean, 'Here lies the heart of Balengus of the Ordovices'. The stone seems to have been moved: it was recorded in 1695 as being close to the church, but it is now in a nearby field.

The magnificent beach, almost a mile long, is owned by the National Trust. At the northern end is a flat rock, called Carreg Morwynion (Maiden's rock), where according to the writings of Samuel Lewis in 1833 'several females have been drowned while bathing there'. At the beach edge there is a turning circle and dropping off point for disabled visitors, and the main car park is some 400 metres inland at Llanborth Farm. The farm was at one time a manor house belonging to the family of Rhys ab Rhydderch, Lord of Tywyn.

Being so remote, the beach was an ideal destination in the 18th century for goods smuggled in from France and Ireland, contraband that would include tobacco, tea, French wine, and spirits and salt from Wicklow. The valley

223

leading down to the beach is called Cwm Lladron, meaning Robbers' Valley.

[It was on the hillside to the right of the picture that Bond and Jinx were to play with Graves' stash of diamonds in the specially constructed beach hut]

No doubt it was the remoteness and beauty of the spot that led the *Die Another Day* production team to film the final scene here. The establishing shot is filmed from a helicopter as it comes around the northern headland, almost at sea level, before swooping up to reveal a beach hut, with helicopter parked outside, on the hillside above the main beach. The turning circle and dropping off point are carefully kept out of view, and with the addition of some foliage as set dressing Penbryn makes a convincing substitute for the South Korean location where we find Bond and Jinx playing with their haul of diamonds.

JAMES BOND IN GWYNEDD
BEDDGELERT - CYM DYLI PIPELINE

[The 'Chapel in the valley' with the King pipeline in the background]

Beddgelert claims to be Snowdonia's loveliest village, with its stone buildings surrounded by the finest scenery in North Wales. The beautiful Aberglaslyn Pass and the Nant Gwynant valley, comprising wooded vales, rocky slopes and mountain lakes, fill the surrounding countryside. Not far from the village, along the banks of the River Glaslyn, will be found Gelert's Grave, which according to legend marks the resting place of Gelert, the faithful hound of the medieval Welsh Prince Llewelyn the Great. The story, as written on the tombstone, reads:

'In the 13th century Llewelyn, prince of North Wales, had a palace at Beddgelert. One day he went hunting without Gelert, 'The Faithful Hound', who was unaccountably absent. On Llewelyn's return the truant, stained and smeared with blood, joyfully sprang to meet his master. The prince alarmed hastened to find his son, and saw the infant's cot empty, the bedclothes and floor covered with blood. The frantic father plunged his sword into the hound's side, thinking it had killed his heir. The dog's dying yell was answered by a child's cry. Llewelyn searched and discovered his boy unharmed, but near by lay the body of a mighty wolf which Gelert had slain. The prince filled with remorse is said never to have smiled again. He buried Gelert here'.

However, the whole thing is most likely a fraud invented to promote tourism by the landlord of the local hotel in the late 18th century, since there is no other evidence to suggest that Gelert ever existed.

225

James Bond in Gwynedd

The village could be said, though, to be the home of Rupert Bear, since Alfred Bestall lived here in a cottage at the foot of Mynydd Sygun and wrote, as well as illustrated, some of the stories while in residence.

The A498, heading north from the village, runs parallel with the River Glaslyn (Afon Glaslyn in Welsh). You first pass, on your right, the Sygun Copper Mine, a major tourist attraction in the area, and shortly after, on the same side, a beautiful lake, Llyn Dinas. Not long after that, on the left, the equally lovely Llyn Gwynant. Also on the left, as the road climbs ever up, are fine views of Mount Snowdon. There are several stopping areas to pull in and admire the views, and it is from these that the Cym Dyli hydro-electric power station and pipeline can be observed. The station was built in 1905, becoming operational in 1906, by the Porthmadog, Beddgelert and South Snowdon Railway to supply electricity to its own railway and connected local slate quarries and mines. Construction was hard work, since three traction engines were needed to help mule and horse teams haul the heavy machinery and other supplies the eight miles over the Llanberis pass from the railway station.

The South Snowdon Railway ran short of money and was never completed, but the electricity generated was used to power Marconi's pioneering transatlantic radio transmitting station at Waunfawr, which became operational in 1914. Today the plant supplies the National Grid, and is Britain's oldest working power station, with just one turbine producing around ten megawatts of electricity.

The building looks less like a power station than a church or school, and it is in fact known locally as the 'Chapel in the valley'. The water for the site is collected from lake Llydaw, on the slopes of Mount Snowdon, some three hundred-and-twenty metres above the power station, and carried from the lake through a one-and-a-quarter mile long pipeline. Rainfall in the area is way above the national average at around thirteen feet per year, so the site was well chosen.

As a water pipeline looks much the same as an oil pipeline on screen, all the establishing shots in *The World Is Not Enough* of the King pipeline passing through Azerbaijan were actually shot at Cwm Dyli. However, the action sequence, in which a section of the pipeline is blown up, apparently killing Bond and Dr Christmas Jones, was filmed in Surrey (page 178).

James Bond on Location Maps

The following maps show the relative positions of the various locations covered in the text. The associated tables give both the type of place, according to the defined symbols below, and the page number in brackets for that location. It is hoped that the maps will help readers in planning their own visits to these places of James Bond interest.

Key to Symbols

	Building (large or important)		Building (general place or structure)		Church (religious establishment)
	Military Establishment		Natural Feature (park or garden)		Tourist Attraction (museum)
	Transport Related				

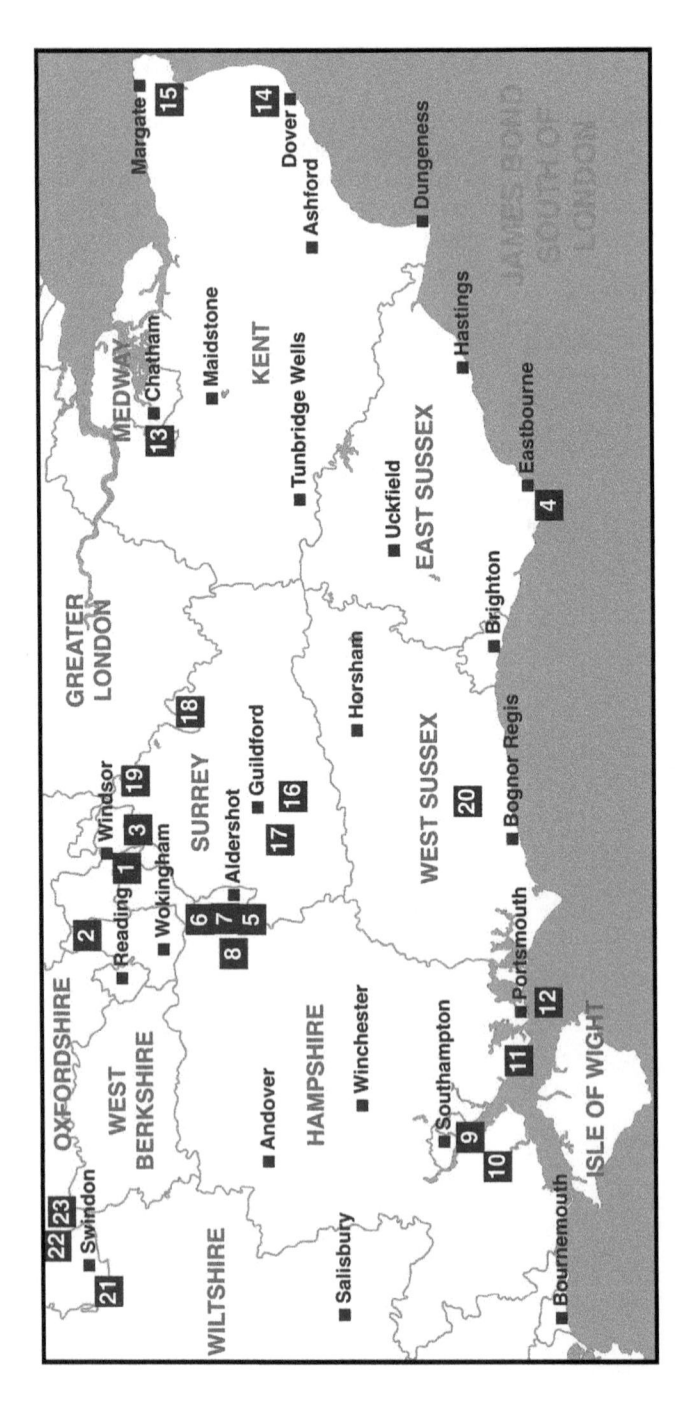

JAMES BOND SOUTH OF LONDON

GREATER LONDON

KENT
- Margate [15]
- Dover [14]
- Ashford
- Dungeness
- Maidstone
- Chatham [13]
- **MEDWAY**
- Tunbridge Wells

EAST SUSSEX
- Hastings
- Eastbourne [4]
- Uckfield
- Brighton

WEST SUSSEX
- Horsham
- Bognor Regis [20]

SURREY
- Guildford [18]
- Aldershot [16]
- [17]

OXFORDSHIRE

WEST BERKSHIRE
- Windsor [19]
- Reading [3]
- Wokingham [1]
- [2]
- [6] [7] [5]
- [8]

HAMPSHIRE
- Andover
- Winchester
- Southampton [11]
- Portsmouth [12]
- [9] [10]

ISLE OF WIGHT

WILTSHIRE
- Swindon [22][23]
- [21]
- Salisbury
- Bournemouth

228

	BERKSHIRE				KENT	
1	Ascot (21)			13	Chatham (129)	
2	Hurley (24)			14	Dover (131)	
3	Wraysbury (26)			15	Manston (134)	
	EAST SUSSEX				SURREY	
4	Beachy Head (93)			16	Cranleigh (175)	
	HAMPSHIRE			17	Elstead (178)	
5	Aldershot (105 & 106)			18	Epsom (181)	
6	Camberley (108)			19	Stanwell (182)	
7	Farnborough (109)				WEST SUSSEX	
8	Odiham (111)			20	Amberley (185)	
9	Southampton (113)				WILTSHIRE	
10	Beaulieu (116)			21	Swindon (191 & 192)	
11	Lee-on-the-Solent (120)			22	Highworth (194)	
12	Portsmouth (122)			23	Sevenhampton (195 & 196)	

229

230

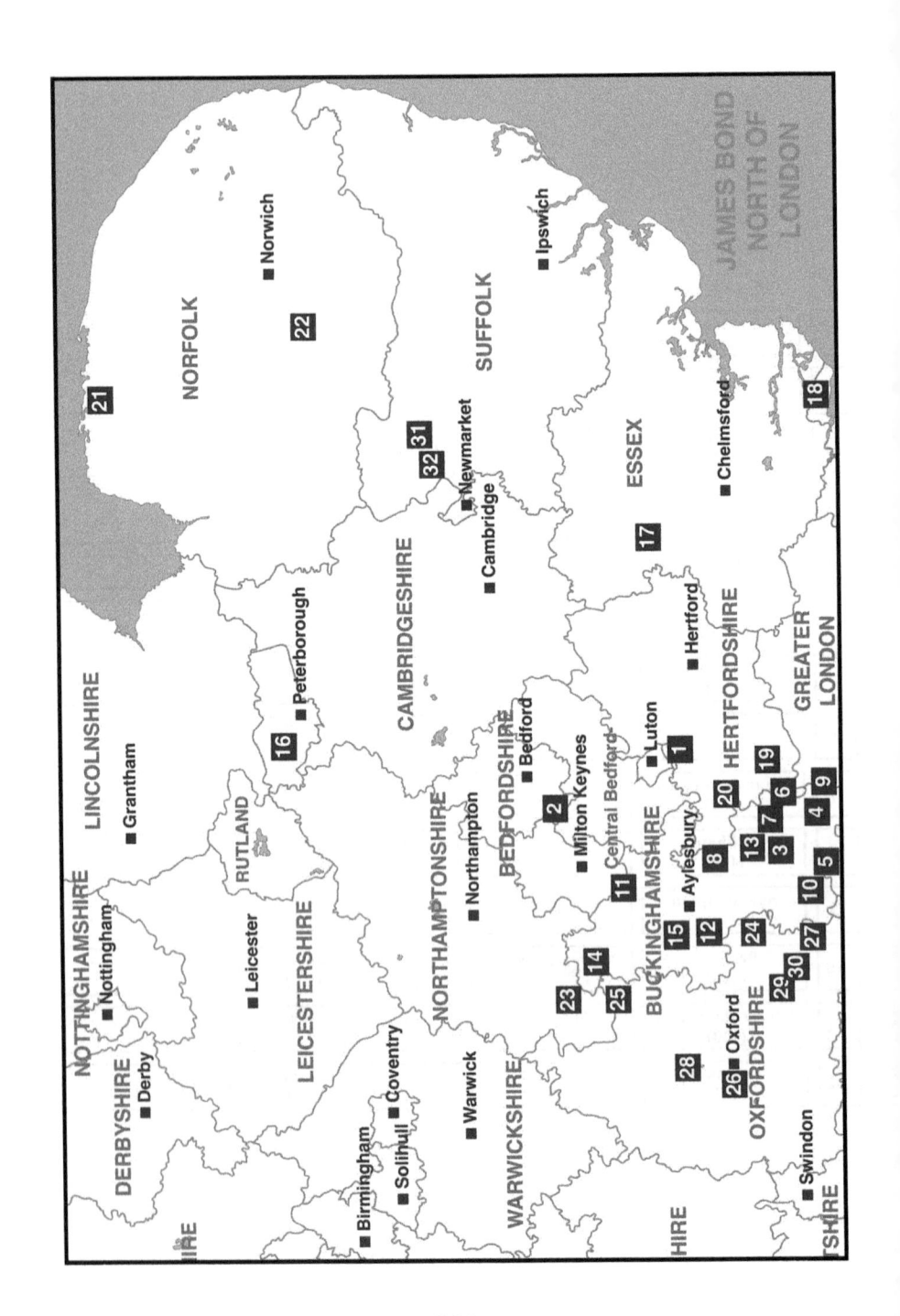

BEDFORDSHIRE

1	Luton (15)		18	Southend-on-Sea (100)	
2	Millbrook (17)				

HERTFORDSHIRE

			19	Abbots Langley (125)	

BUCKINGHAMSHIRE

3	Beaconsfield (29)		20	Bovingdon (126)	
4	Black Park (31)				

NORFOLK

5	Burnham Beeches (37)		21	Burnham Deepdale (137)	
6	Denham (39)		22	Snetterton (139)	
7	Gerrards Cross (41)				

NORTHAMPTONSHIRE

8	Halton (42)		23	Silverstone (141)	
9	Iver Heath (45)				

OXFORDSHIRE

10	Marlow (56)		24	Chinnor (143)	
11	Newport Pagnell (58)		25	Finmere (145)	
12	Oakley (62)		26	Oxford (146 & 148)	
13	Stoke Poges (64 & 66)		27	Stonor (151 & 154)	
14	Stowe (69)		28	Upper Heyford (155)	
15	Waddesdon (72)		29	Drayton St. Leonard (164)	
			30	Nettlebed (165)	

CAMBRIDGESHIRE

16	Wansford (75)				

SUFFOLK

			31	Elveden (169)	

ESSEX

17	Stanstead Mountfitchet (97)		32	Lakenheath (171)	

231

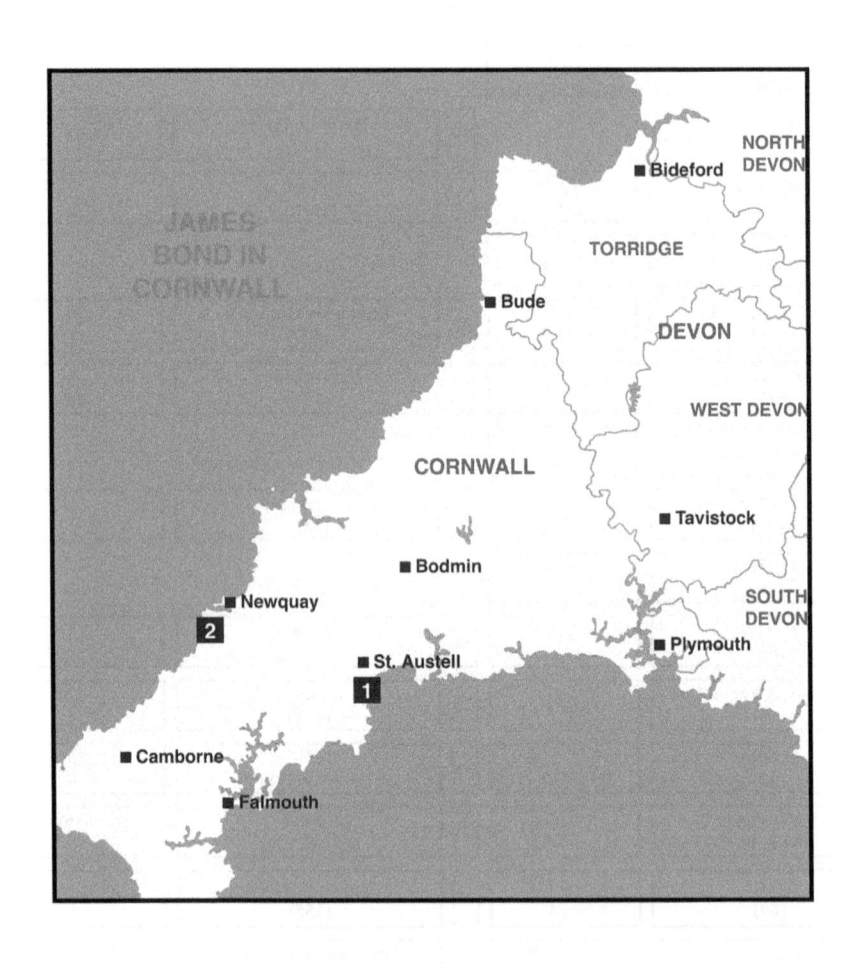

CORNWALL

| 1 | Bodelva (89) | | 2 | Newquay (91) | |

JAMES
BOND IN
WALES

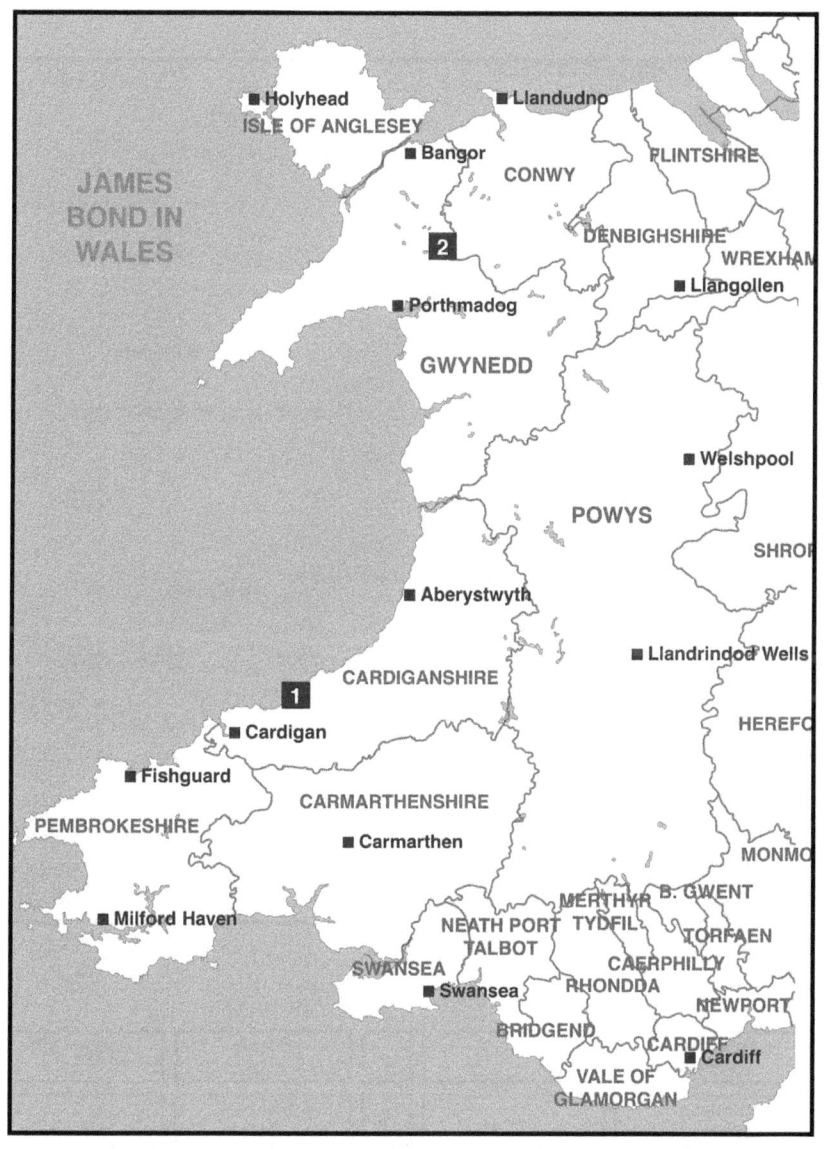

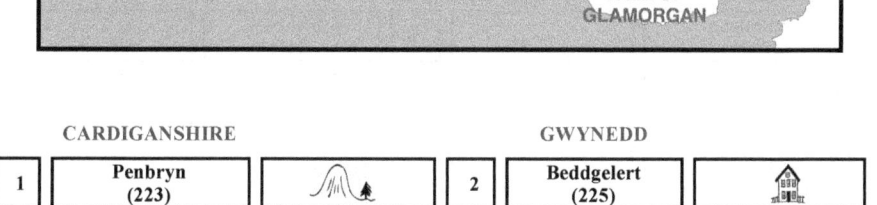

	CARDIGANSHIRE			GWYNEDD	
1	Penbryn (223)	🏔	2	Beddgelert (225)	🏠

233

JAMES BOND IN SCOTLAND

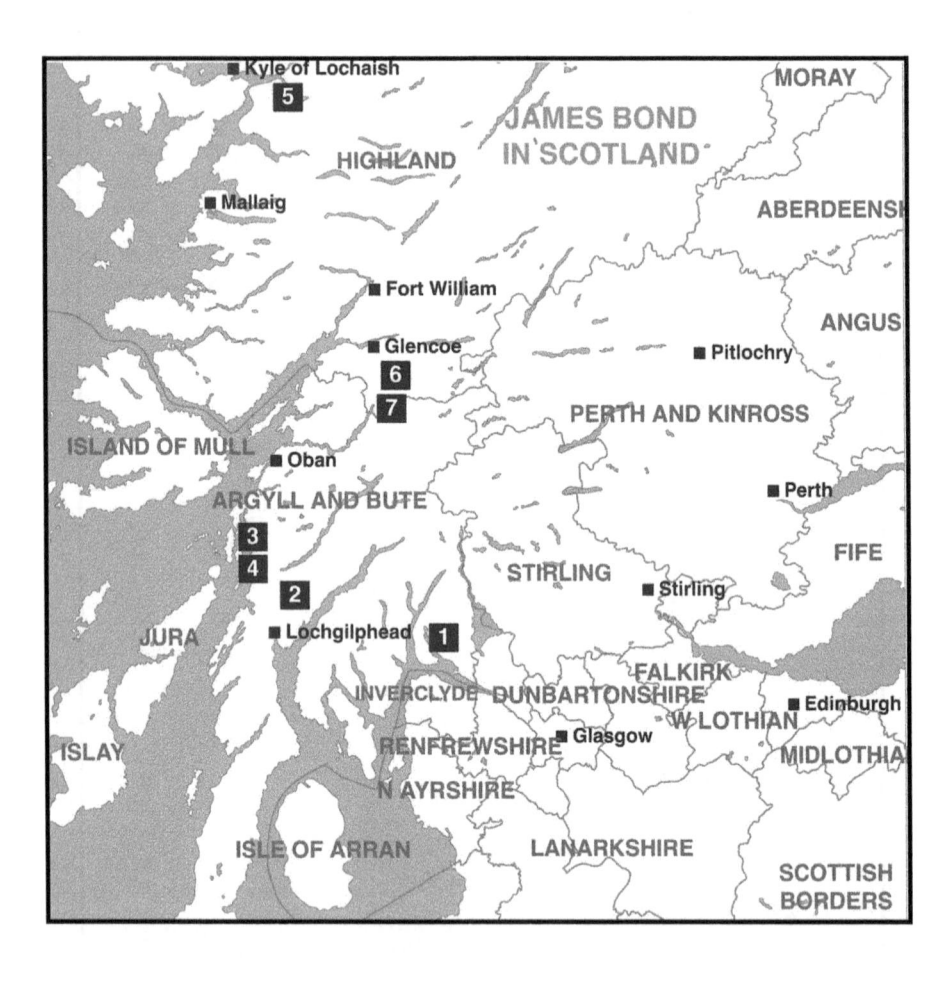

	ARGYLL & BUTE				HIGHLAND	
1	Garelochhead (199)			5	Dornie (213)	
2	Kilmichael Glassary (201)			8	Glencoe (215)	
3	Loch Craignish (204, 206 & 208)			9	Dalness (219)	
4	Duntrune (211)					

234

PLACES INDEX

Buildings – Large or Important (Non Tourist Attractions)
Ascot Racecourse 21
Brasenose College 146
Duntrune Castle 211
Eleveden Hall 169
Epsom Downs Racecourse 181
Joyce Grove 165
Luton Hoo 15
New College 148
Pinewood Studios 45
Sevenhampton Place 195
Spectrum Building 191
Stoke Park 66
Vygon (ex Motorola) Building 192

Buildings – General Places or Structures
Chalfont Park House 41
Cym Dyli Pipeline 225
Dalness Lodge 219
Deepdale Farm 137
Esso West London Terminal 182
Goldfinger Tavern 194
Lunga Pier 204
Royal Saracen's Head Hotel 29
Snetterton Park Models 139
Thames Lawn 56
Whitepond Farm 154

Churches or Other Ecclesiastical Buildings
St. Giles' Church 64
St. James' Church 196

Military Establishments
Bruneval Barracks 105
Eelmoor Driver Training Area (Long Valley) 106
Halton House 42
H.M. Naval Base Clyde 199
Minley Training Area 108
Portsmouth Naval Base 122
R.A.F. Lakenheath 171
R.A.F. Oakley 62
R.A.F. Odiham 111
R.A.F. Upper Heyford 155

Places Index

Natural Features – Parks or Gardens (Non Tourist Attractions)
Barrachuile 201
Beachy Head 93
Black Park 31
Burnham Beeches 37
Chinnor Chalk Quarries 143
Craobh Haven 208
Crinan 206
Denham Quarry Lakes 39
Glen Etive 215
Hankley Common 178
Holywell Bay 91
Hurley Lock 24
Penbryn Beach 223
Wraysbury Lake 26

Tourist Attractions
Amberley Museum & Heritage Centre 185
Aston Martin Heritage Trust 164
Eden Project 89
Eilean Donan Castle 213
Historic Dockyard Chatham, The 129
Hovercraft Museum, The 120
Leavesden Studios 125
National Motor Museum, Beaulieu 116
Nene Valley Railway 75
Stonor Park 151
Stowe Landscape Gardens 69
Waddesdon Manor 72

Transport Related (Non Military and Non Tourist Attractions)
Aston Martin Works 58
Bovingdon Airfield 126
Dunsfold Aerodrome 175
Farnborough Airport 109
Finmere Airport 145
Kent International Airport 134
London Southend Airport 100
Millbrook Proving Ground 17
Port of Dover Ferry Terminal 131
Silverstone Circuit 141
Southampton Docks 113
Stansted Airport 97

FILM INDEX

Dr. No (1962)
10, 46, 209

From Russia With Love (1963)
10, 26, 48-51, 53, 54, 118, 201-203, 204-210

Goldfinger (1964)
9, 10, 32, 36, 38, 51-54, 60, 66-68, 100-103, 118-119, 148, 183-184, 194

Thunderball (1965)
9, 30, 40-41, 42, 60, 61, 103, 142

You Only Live Twice (1967)
10, 54, 118-119, 146, 151, 219

On Her Majesty's Secret Service (1969)
10, 56, 57, 61, 65

Diamonds Are Forever (1971)
10, 58, 61, 81, 114-115, 121, 132-134

Live and Let Die (1973)
52

The Man with the Golden Gun (1974)
10, 127-128

The Spy Who Loved Me (1977)
9, 10, 55, 118, 199-200

Moonraker (1979)
11, 48, 63

For Your Eyes Only (1981)
9, 55, 65-66

Octopussy (1983)
9, 32, 33, 54, 55, 62, 63, 75, 77-85, 118, 155-163

Never Say Never Again **(1983)**
9, 16, 73-74

A View to a Kill **(1985)**
10, 22-24, 27, 55, 185-189, 191-192

The Living Daylights **(1987)**
9, 10, 62, 94-95, 151, 153-154, 171

Licence to Kill **(1989)**
48

GoldenEye **(1995)**
10, 24, 48, 60, 86-87, 126, 139-140, 181-182

Tomorrow Never Dies **(1997)**
11, 48, 67, 99-100, 122-123, 148, 150, 173

The World Is Not Enough **(1999)**
16, 32, 42, 44-45, 53, 54, 60, 70-71, 129-131, 179, 193, 213-214, 226

Die Another Day **(2002)**
10, 53, 54, 55, 62, 90, 91, 106-107, 109, 113, 121, 135-136, 137-138, 144, 223-224

Casino Royale **(2006)**
9, 10, 18, 32, 34, 48, 55, 60, 62, 175-177

Quantum of Solace **(2008)**
55, 62, 106, 111, 177

Skyfall **(2012)**
9, 10, 11, 24, 55, 60, 99, 178-180, 182, 212, 217-218, 219

ACKNOWLEDGMENTS

The author and publisher are delighted to be able to thank all those who have supported this publication from its inception.

With the exception of those listed below all photographs in this book were either already in the public domain, or were taken by the author. Our thanks is given to all those who have graciously given permission for their photographs to be used here.

Amberley Museum & Heritage Centre (pages 186-189), Aston Martin Heritage Trust (page 58), Can Stock Photo Inc. (gun barrel image), Crown Copyright Reserved (pages 42, 112, 123, 172 and 200), Deepdale Farms (page 137), Dunsfold Park (page 175), the Eden Project (pages 89-90), The Hovercraft Museum Trust (pages 106-107), the Man family (page 57), Millbrook Proving Ground Limited (page 17), The National Motor Museum at Beaulieu (Bond in Motion exhibition) (pages 19, 28, 33, 61, 64, 118-119, 176-177 and 207), Stephen Norris (page 91), Octane (Aston Martin at Glencoe), Photoshot (Daniel Craig image), Simplon Postcards (page 115), Arthur E. Sevigny (pages 155 and 157-162), Ranjit Singh (pages 169-170), Joan Street (page 72) and Surrey Life (pages 178-179).

Special thanks goes to Stephen Norris who has given his boundless knowledge and advice freely in all aspects of this book, and also to Graham Rye (editor, designer and publisher of 007 Magazine) for his input, along with Roger Johnson for his editing and proof reading skills. In alphabetical order the following are also thanked for their generous time, advice and expertise; Donna K. Bannister (Aston Martin Heritage Trust), Andrew Beach (Millbrook Proving Ground Limited), James Borthwick (Deepdale Farms), Ian Boyle (Simplon Postcards), Tony Burlton (Landmarc Support Services Limited), Dr. Heather Dix, Ally Davies (Amberley Museum & Heritage Centre), Mark Dixon (Octane), Nancy Edwards (Dunsfold Park), Flight Lieutenant Shazia Higgins (R.A.F. Halton), Warwick Jacobs (The Hovercraft Museum Trust), Marilyn Jenner (Nene Valley Railway), David Lillywhite (Octane), Niven MacVicar, Ronnie McLennan, Sarah Parry (Elveden Hall), Ben Pratt (The Hovercraft Museum Trust), James Richards, Charles Salkield (Wraysbury Lake Sailing Club), Mrs. P. A. Stephens (Inflite), Don Todd (Heyford Park Management Company Limited), Jane Townsend-Emms (Octane), Varshana Trudgian (Eden Project), Matthew Williams (Surrey Life), David Win (Eilean Donan Castle) and Sarah Wright (Beaulieu Enterprises Limited).

Acknowledgments

References used in the research of this book, and highly recommended to those who would like to explore the themes of this publication further include:

Cork, John & Stutz, Collin, *James Bond Encyclopedia*, 336 pages, Dorling Kindersley Limited, (2009), ISBN: 978-1-40534-430-2.

Mulder, Martijn & Kloosterboer, Dirk, *On The Tracks of 007*, 287 pages, DMD Digital, (2008), ISBN: 978-0-97131-330-9.

Finally, at a corporate level gratitude goes to the Crinan Hotel, Lunga Estates, National Trust, EON, Danjaq, United Artists Corporation, Columbia Pictures Industries, Sony, MGM, the Ian Fleming Estate and of course the late Ian Fleming himself for originally creating the character of James Bond without which this publication would not exist.

**THE END OF *JAMES BOND ON LOCATION*
VOLUME 2: U.K. (excluding LONDON)**

**BUT *JAMES BOND ON LOCATION* WILL RETURN
IN VOLUME 3 DEDICATED TO THE
EUROPEAN FILMING LOCATIONS**